Drea...

Celebrity Book of
DREAMS

Dreamland's

Celebrity Book of
DREAMS

**Dreams of the Famous
and what your Dreams mean to you**

Migene González-Wippler, Charles Alverson
and others

Quiller Press · London

Dreamland Appliances Limited is the United King-
dom's leading manufacturer of electric blankets. The
company is based in Minstead, Hants and is part of the
multinational Yale and Valor group of companies.
Dreamland products are sold in dozens of countries
around the world and the company is renowned for its
innovative products and reliability.

Yale and Valor Small Appliances
Castle Malwood House
Minstead
Nr. Lyndhurst
Tel: (0703) 813999   *Hants SO43 7NA*

First published in 1989 by
Quiller Press Ltd
46 Lillie Road
London SW6 1TN

Illustrated by Robert Kendall
Front cover illustration came from Image Bank, London

Copyright © 1989 – Chapters 1–7: Migene González-Wippler
Dream Dictionary: Charles Alverson

ISBN 1 870948 27 0

Designed by Dale Dawson

Design and production in association with
Book Production Consultants, 47 Norfolk Street, Cambridge

Typeset by Textype Typesetters

Printed by Richard Clay Ltd, Bungay, Suffolk

Contents

Throughout:
Celebrity Dreams, Dream Sayings of the Famous, Dream Lore, Science of Dreams, Children's Dreams.

The Publishers would particularly like to thank the thirty-eight celebrities – as well as the six primary school children – who have contributed so generously to this book, the royalities of which go to The Royal National Institute for the Blind.

Eric Newby's contribution comes from Love and War in the Appenines
(Hodder & Stoughton)

Foreword:
The blind dream

John Wall, Vice-Chairman RNIB

'Paint me a picture!' demands John Mortimer's blind father of his son in that brilliant, loving, dramatic portrait *A Voyage Round my Father*. It is a cry from the heart. Most blind people once had their sight, and can and do visualise what is going on around them. Those few who have been blind from birth quickly become aware of their environment and can picture what it is like.

So in their waking hours blind people have vivid mental images of what their sighted peers can see, and it follows that when they dream they 'see' pictures. Of course in dreams nobody, sighted or blind, 'sees'. The eyes are shut and out of action.

I suppose some blind people must have dreamt that they have recovered their sight and recently blinded people will see into their dreams pictures of what they saw when they had their sight.

Indeed, this is not confined to recently blinded people. My sight failed in 1938 when I was eight years old. I now live in Surrey but I was born and bred in Finchley. Last night (late August 1989) I had a dream which it would be tedious to recount in detail. But it is worth mentioning that at one point I was walking up the Bishop's Avenue (Finchley's millionaires' row) and the red brickwork of the houses looked much as it did when, as a seven-year-old child, I watched the navvies making up the road.

Someone will now tell me that the brickwork of the houses in the Bishop's Avenue is not red, or even that no brickwork is visible on what the surveyors rather pompously call 'the front elevations'. That doesn't matter. I intend to hold on to my picture.

Dreams are, of course, a mish-mash of factual and fictional memories, hopes and fears for the future, warnings and promises from the subconscious. I don't think the dreams which blind people experience are much different from those of the sighted. Returning to consciousness is, of course, different for a blind person. Living with your eyes permanently shut differs from having the option to open them.

I have found the proofs of this book fascinating. It covers all aspects of dreams and dreaming. It makes its points in language readily intelligible to the uninstructed layman. It deserves to become a bestseller.

John Wall
August 1989

Sweet dreams

Dreamland Appliances are in the business of ensuring that their customers sleep warm, safe and comfortable during the colder winter months. We hope that sleeping in comfort will ensure sweet and pleasant dreams and for this reason we felt that a book about dreams was very appropriate for our company. We are delighted to know that we will also be helping the RNIB, a very worthwhile organisation, who will benefit directly from the sales of the book. The book, we are sure, will be of immense interest to everyone, for all of us at some time have had dreams that have puzzled, disturbed or even frightened us and we would have loved to have known the meaning of them. Now the *Dreamland Celebrity Book of Dreams* may provide the answer. The book is absorbing, humorous and enlightening – an enjoyable read for all the family.

Dreamland
September 1989

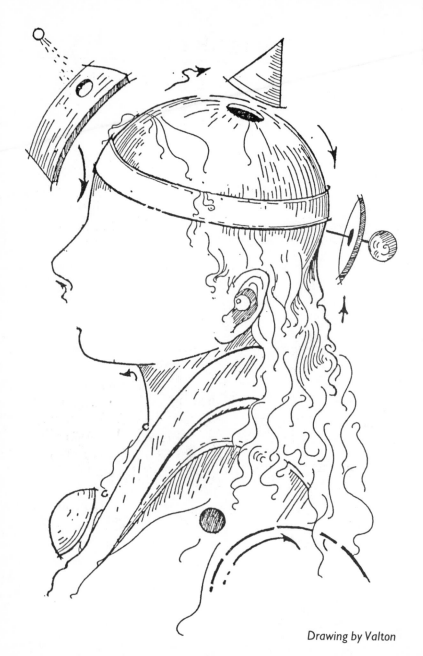

Drawing by Valton

Part I
Dreams and the Human Mind

Migene González-Wippler

The Author

Migene González-Wippler was born in Puerto Rico and has degrees in psychology and anthropology from the University of Puerto Rico and from Columbia University. She has worked as a science editor for the Interscience Division of John Wiley, the American Institute of Physics and the American Museum of Natural History in New York, and as an English editor for the United Nations in Vienna, where she lived for many years. She is the noted author of many books on religion and mysticism.

1. Understanding the Human Mind

*I believe it to be true that dreams are
the true interpretation of our inclinations;
but there is art required to sort and understand them*
– Montaigne, *Essays II*, xii

Since his early beginnings man has been fascinated by the mysteries of his own mind. He has tried to penetrate the intricate labyrinths of his mental processes in myriad ways. But still, even today, in spite of the many discoveries and advances in the field of psychology, man still asks himself the eternal question: *What is mind?*

Plato's Definition of Mind
Many great intellects have endeavoured to answer this question. Plato defined mind as a God-given spiritual quality that was totally separated from what he called the 'gross material body.' Our physical senses – sight, touch and hearing – often deceive us. But through reason, rooted in mind, we may arise at true knowledge and understanding. To Plato, reason was a vehicle by means of which our sensorial experiences and memories of past experiences could be used as materials for a process of synthesis, analysis and classification that would help us to understand the world around us. Ideas, a term coined by Plato, were certain qualities or essences of mind which we learned to identify as 'permanent realities,' and which constantly imparted their unchanging form and character to our transient lives on earth. Among such ideas, he cited beauty, truth, faith, hope, and all abstract thoughts.

2

Aristotle's Argument

Plato's famous disciple, Aristotle, had somewhat different views from his great master. To Aristotle, the body had mysterious psychic powers, which he associated with the existence of the soul in man. By soul he meant the vital energy that is present in all living things. In its most primitive aspect, the **nutritive** soul, it keeps all live bodies feeding, growing and reproducing their kind. As the **sensitive** soul, it feels emotions and sensations and is the seat of memory. Finally, as the **reasonable** soul, it thinks, judges and reasons. It is mind. Therefore, Aristotle, unlike Plato, believed that both the senses and the mind had a common link in the human soul. But both Plato and Aristotle agreed on one basic thing; the awesome powers of the mind.

After the death of Aristotle, nearly two thousand years elapsed before another great philosopher decided to find new answers to the question of mind. This was René Descartes, undoubtedly the greatest of French philosophers.

Descartes' Discussion

Descartes, best known for his famous statement, 'I think, therefore I am,' redefined thinking as the whole range of conscious mental processes, including feelings, sensations, intellectual thoughts and will. He deepened the division that Plato had made between mind and body by insisting that sensation was a function of the mind rather than of the body. In fact, Descartes believed that all of

The French philosopher, René Descartes (1596–1660) discovered the foundations of his '*Discourse of Method*' through a revelation he had in dreams when he was twenty-three. He considered this to be supernatural inspiration.

man's animating processes were controlled by the mind. His most daring theory was that the mind had 'innate' ideas it was born with. He also believed that the mind is always at work, even during sleep.

Descartes' theories created a veritable beehive of controversy among the scholars of the time. Some like John Locke, totally rejected them. Others, like Baruch Spinoza, accepted them, albeit guardedly.

Of all Descartes' contemporaries, Spinoza was perhaps the most important because of the influence he was to have centuries later on one of the most innovative thinkers of all times, Sigmund Freud.

The Science of Dreams

The scientific theory of dreams started with the Greeks, Plato and Aristotle. In Plato's *Republic*, Socrates says: 'In all of us, even in good men, there is a lawless, wild-beast nature which peers out in sleep.'

Aristotle also thought that dreams could transform small stimuli into the sensation of great stimuli: '.... men think it is lightning and thundering, when there are only faint echoes in their ears, and that they are enjoying honey and sweet flavours, when only a drop of phlegm is slipping down their throats, and that they are walking through fire and are tremendously hot when there is only a slight heating about certain parts.'

The Birth of Psychology

When Freud was born in Austria in 1856, the science of psychology was in its infancy. It had been born barely six years before, on 22 October 1850, when a German professor named Gustav Theodor Fechner decided that the mind and its relation to matter could be scientifically measured. Ten years later, Fechner wrote his famous work, *Elements of Psychophysics*, where he gave the world his technique on how to measure mental processes.

Fechner's studies were followed by those of Wilhelm Wundt, whose prime interest was in sensation. Wundt conducted numerous experiments during which he attempted to break down experience into elements of sensation. During these experiments, students in his laboratory stared at flashing lights, listened to metronomes and pricked each other with needles. Their purpose was to analyse what they heard, saw and felt. Wundt's first important work, *Principles of Physiological Psychology*, was published in 1874.

The pioneer work of Fechner and Wundt was followed by many scientists on both sides of the Atlantic. In the United States, William James, the illustrious brother of the novelist Henry James, turned his attention to the human consciousness, which he described as both continuous and selective. His great book, *The Principles of Psychology*, which he published in 1890, is still used as a college textbook.

Division Develops

By the middle of the 1910s, two schools of experimental psychology had been developed. One was the American school of Behaviourism. The other was the German Gestalt school. The Behaviourists believed that the study of man's actions can help understand the reasons for his behaviour, thereby shedding light on his mental processes. The Gestalt psychologists, on the other hand, dealt with perception. Their main thesis was that we always tend to perceive the whole before we perceive its parts. This led them to believe that immediate, meaningful perception is arrived at by the mind's ability to create relationships. Thus, we learn a song's tune before we learn the notes and perceive the form and the beauty of a rose before we become aware of its petals, its stem and its leaves.

The Behaviourism and the Gestalt schools are still active at present, and although their approaches to the

> The first man to make the study of dreams his main work was Artemidorus of Daldi (c. 140 AD) who lived under the Roman Emperor Antoninus Pius. He classified the incidents of sleep as: dreams, visions, oracles, fantasies and apparitions, each with its own separate and distinct function. The function of dreams, he said, was to discover the truth in a symbolic image.
>
> According to Artemidorus, 'Those who are skilled in interpretation discern their wishes through the veil of symbols.'

study of mind are completely different, they often blend their varied points of views.

Freud's Unconscious

While the Behaviourist and the Gestalt pyschologists were concerned with the workings of the conscious mind, in Vienna, Freud was deeply involved with the study of *the deep unconscious mind*. After graduating as a doctor in 1885, Freud had gone to Paris for a while to study hypnosis under the supervision of the famed teacher and neurologist Jean-Marie Charcot. Freud's interest in Charcot's methods was primarily directed at the Frenchman's use of hypnosis in the treatment of hysteria.

When Freud returned to Vienna, he began in earnest the development of his theories about the unconscious. After a short and abortive attempt at work in collaboration with Josef Breuer, a fellow physician, he set out to work alone on his belief that emotions and unconscious motivations were the prime movers of our lives, rather than intelligence. These ideas, as well as his belief in the importance of infantile sexuality in the development of the personality, alienated a great number of his colleagues, who believed that man was essentially a rational being. For a while, Freud found himself ostracised from the rest of the scientific community, but his faith in his theories never wavered, and eventually the world had to recognize the importance of his contributions to the field of psychology.

Freud's Repression

Freud believed that the average individual rejects all hostile and destructive impulses, as well as socially unacceptable forms of sexual gratification. These antisocial urges are very distasteful to acknowledge by the conscious self of a civilised human being. Awareness of these urges arouses anxiety in the individual, who blocks the negative impulses by means of a process which Freud called 'repression.'

Freud's Sex Drive

The theory of repression was followed by Freud's theory on human sexuality. He called the sexual instinct 'libido,' and pointed out that the sexual life of an individual begins at the moment of birth. In his view, a person's libido could be satisfied in many ways, such as strenuous physical activity, sports and creative outlets. The libido is often repressed because of the demands of society upon an individual. This creates great conflict within the personality. Thus, other outlets have to be found to ease the anxiety the repressed sexual instinct causes to the individual.

Freud believed that the sexual instinct was one of two major drives in the personality. The second drive was the

---

Sigmund Freud (1856–1939), the Austrian originator of psychoanalysis, believed that the mind acted as a censor and that dreams were the first line of defence of sleep in that they altered the dreamer's thoughts to those which would not disturb sleep.

Freud considered his work on the interpretation of dreams (1899) his most important achievement and still thought this even thirty-two years later.

self-preservation instinct. These two drives he combined into one urge, the 'life instinct', which he called 'Eros'. He believed that the life instinct was able to divert another basic drive, the 'death instinct', away from the individual concerned and direct it instead towards others in the form of outward 'aggression'.

The Id, Ego and Superego

Further observation of human personality, especially in battle-shocked soldiers, led Freud to suggest the personality division which was to form the backbone of Freudian psychology. In this division, Freud saw the human personality formed of three closely interrelated parts: the **Id**, the **Ego** and the **Superego**.

The **Id** is totally unconscious, and is composed of primitive urges and instincts that seek gratification without regard to the consequences to the individual.

The **Ego** is the conscious part of the personality and stands between the Id and the real world and acts as a mediator between the two.

The **Superego** is partly conscious, and urges the individual to resist the negative impulses of the Id and practice instead the highest and most noble of human ideals. It acts in a sense as a 'conscience', and judges severely between good and bad behaviour. Obedience to

---

A skilful man reads dreams for his self-knowledge...Wise and sometimes terrible hints shall in them (dreams) be thrown to the man out of a quite unknown intelligence. He shall be startled two or three times in his life by the justice as well as the significance of this phantasmagoria. Once or twice the conscious fetters shall seem to be unlocked, and a freer utterance attained.

– *Ralph Waldo Emerson (1803–82), American poet and essayist*

'Dreams and visions are infused into men for their advantage and instruction.'

— *Artemidorus of Daldi (c. 140 AD), Roman dream interpreter*

the impulses of the Superego promotes feelings of happiness and well-being, while disobedience makes the individual feel guilty and worthless.

The Ego's Function

The Ego, caught between the conflicting demands of the Id and the Superego, undergoes severe tensions and conflict. The result of this struggle and how it affects the Ego is what forms the human personality. When the Ego is successful in harmonising the urges of the Id and the Superego, the result is a healthy, well-balanced personality. When the Ego fails in harmonising them, the personality can be damaged and a neurosis or acute anxiety will follow. If the damage is so extreme that the Ego can no longer function, psychosis of mental illness is the result.

The repressed impulses of both the Id and the Superego continually strive for expression and gratification, thus exerting a strong, powerful influence on the personality. The individual cannot describe these impulses but they surface in disguised symbolic imagery in slips of the tongue, lapses of memory and in dreams.

Dreams as Clues to the Unconscious

Freud was quick to realise that dreams could give him invaluable clues to the repressed feelings that caused a psychological disorder in a patient. He eventually evolved a theory that explained that dreams are the best possible record of the human unconscious. The reason why dreams are always symbolic in essence, according to Freud, is that very often they represent an unconscious wish that is socially unacceptable or too frightening or unpleasant to be allowed into outer consciousness, even in the form of a dream. Therefore, they are disguised in symbolic form. In this way, they can be released from the unconscious, relieving it of anxiety and repression, without offending the sensibilities of the outward, conscious personality.

Free Association

In the beginning of his psychological practice, Freud used the techniques of hypnosis he learned from Charcot, but soon he realised this system had too many inadequacies that hindered his progress. Some of his patients could not be hypnotised at all. Those who could be did not always respond to his suggestions. This led Freud to search for an alternative approach to the unconscious, until he eventually developed a technique he called 'free association'. His patients were asked to lie down on a couch in Freud's study and talk about the first thing that came to their minds. Freud discovered he could trace strong emotional drives and the sources of mental anxieties and neuroses in the often disconnected ramblings of his patients. This was to be birth of psychoanalysis.

Dreams, however, remained the main source of information on the hidden workings of the human unconscious. In 1900, Freud published his classic work on the subject, *The Interpretation of Dreams*, which is still in use today by modern psychology.

Jung Joins the Search

Of all Freud's followers, the most famous was Swiss psychiatrist Carl Gustav Jung. Concepts like *extroverted* and *introverted* are some of Jung's lasting contributions to the field of psychology.

Although fascinated by Freud's ideas of the unconscious, Jung soon parted company with Freud because of the latter's great emphasis on sexuality. Jung's doctrines,

Carl Gustav Jung (1875–1961), Swiss psychologist and critic of Freud, urged his patients to keep a careful record of their dreams and of the interpretations given because, he said, "...dreams contain something more than practical helps for the doctor. Dream analysis deserves very special attention. Sometimes, indeed, it is a matter of life and death."

which were to be known eventually as Analytical Psychology, were deeply influenced by myths, mysticism, metaphysics and the religious experience. Freud's work was too materialistic and biological in its orientation and did not agree in principle with Jung's belief in the importance of the historical and spiritual side of man. When Jung published his revolutionary work *Psychology of the Unconscious* in 1912, the formal break between the two great men was completed.

Jung Differs

Jung redefined some of the Freudian terms in the development of his psychology. Ego, for instance, he redefined as the complex of representations which constitutes the centre of an individual's consciousness and which appears to possess a very high degree of continuity and identity. Jung saw the Ego as an 'autonomous complex', which was at the centre of the consciousness. Thus we see that whereas to Freud the Ego formed all the components of the conscious personality, to Jung the Ego is only the focus of personal identity, the **Me**, while the consciousness is the manifestation of the individual's awareness of himself and of the outer world.

Another Freudian term redefined by Jung was *libido*. To Freud, this word meant the entire complex of human sexual impulses. To Jung, it signified the energy of the processes of life. Jung often used two terms interchangeably to describe the energy that operates in the psyche. One of the terms was libido and the other was **psychic energy**. The main difference between Freud and Jung's concept of libido is that Jung works with a larger and more flexible concept of energy. To him, libido or psychic energy has two aspects. One is cosmic energy, the other is energy manifested specifically in the psyche of man.

Consciousness as Defined by Jung

Jung also broke away from Freudian psychology in his concept of the various levels of consciousness. He conceived the psyche as having three layers. At the surface is Consciousness; below it is the Personal Unconscious; and at the base is the Objective or Collective Unconscious.

Consciousness contains the attitudes of the individual, his Ego, his approaches to external environment. It is also the seat of his rational and logical processes. It is not only the face he presents to the world, but also his awareness of that world and how he copes with it.

The Personal Unconscious houses the psychic contents that have been repressed from consciousness either deliberately or unknowingly, as well as those urges that have not yet reached the conscious aspect of the personality. In many ways, the Personal Unconscious resembles Freud's concept of the Id, but Jung conceived of it only as the 'more or less superficial layer of the unconscious.' It contains fantasies, dreams, and ideologies of a personal character, which are the result of personal experiences, things forgotten or repressed.

The Objective of Collective Unconscious is the largest and deepest area of the psyche. Jung believed this part of the human unconscious is the seat of the memories of all humanity, and contains the roots of the four psychological functions: sensation, intuition, thought and feeling.

The Collective Unconscious is the container of all latent memory traces of man's entire history. It is common to all

'If we meditate on a dream sufficiently long and thoroughly, if we carry it around with us and turn it over and over, something almost always comes of it.'

– Carl Gustav Jung

human beings and harbours within all the knowledge and wisdom of the past. Thus, in principle according to Jung, *the human unconscious has all the answers to every possible question about man's beginnings.* All our latent fears, desires and inclinations also come from the Collective Unconscious, and both the Ego and the Personal Unconscious are built upon it.

Archetypes

A large part of the Collective Unconscious consists of those basic components of the human psyche Jung called the **archetypes**. An archetype is a universal concept containing a large element of emotion and myth.

The concept of the archetype is very important in the understanding of dream symbology because it explains why some dream images seem to have a universal meaning that applies to all members of the human race, while other images are highly personalised and concern only each individual dreamer.

Jung conceived the archetype as an 'autonomous complex', that is, a part of the psyche that detaches itself from consciousness to such an extent that it appears to be independent from the rest of the personality and to lead an autonomous life of its own. This in itself is not an abnormal condition, provided it is allowed to highlight only certain aspects of the personality and that the consciousness maintains full control over all the various parts of the psyche.

The main types of autonomous complexes or archetypes conceived by Jung as parts of the psyche are the

The ancient Egyptians divided dreams into three categories:

1. Unsolicited dreams in which the gods appealed to man's conscience, demanding repentance and pity.
2. Warning dreams in which the gods warned the dreamer of dangers ahead.
3. Dreams which were answers to questions put to the gods by the dreamer.

Persona, the Shadow, the Anima and the Animus, and the Self. These archetypes appear in dreams in the form of figures that may or may not be known to the dreamer.

The Persona

The Persona is the mask that the individual wears in his daily life, the face he presents to the outside world. It is, in other words, his conscious personality. The Persona is identified with the Ego, and it appears in dreams in the form of a figure that embodies those qualities that typify the Ego. If the individual is severe in his/her general outlook on life, the Persona may appear in his/her dreams as a stern old man. On the other hand, if the individual is 'devil may care' in his/her attitude, the Persona may be represented by a clown or a child.

Because the Persona represents the individual's conscious attitude, it is placed in the psyche as an opposite of the unconscious. This means the contents of the Persona are in a constantly tense relationship with the unconscious. Any extremes that the individual builds in his persona will be counteracted by opposite extremes in the unconscious. For example if a person presents to the world an overly moral and conservative face, he will suffer great torments from completely opposite unconscious urges. Thus, it is very vital for mental health to endeavour to build a reasonably well-balanced Persona that is harmonious to the individual and not difficult for him/her to maintain.

The Shadow

The Ego tends to develop the strong side of its personality and to integrate it into its conscious attitudes and thus into the Persona. The weaker aspects of the pscyhe are then gathered, unwanted, into the unconscious, and there they form another autonomous complex or archetype known as the Shadow. This is the dark side of the personality, and it surfaces from time to time to embarrass and generally to harass the individual. It appears in the conscious personality without warning, as sudden moods and urges that lead the individual to do and say things that are generally contrary to his usual behaviour. This sometimes happens when the tension between the Persona and the unconscious is so great that large amounts of libido or psychic energy are released by the psyche. This libido left undirected and unchannelled turns back into the unconscious and causes old repressed urges and desires to overflow into the conscious aspects of the psyche. This overflow is the archetype known as the Shadow.

The Shadow Knows

Very often, normal instincts and creative impulses are relegated to the realm of the Shadow along with the negative and destructive side of the Ego. For that reason, it is vital for each individual to accept this darker aspect of his/her personality and try to understand and channel this psychic energy along constructive paths so that it will not overpower his consciousness, threatening his/her normality and well-being.

The interplay between the Ego and the Shadow is not unlike the struggle between Dr Jekyll and Mr Hyde in the Robert Louis Stevenson novel. Thus, we can say that the Shadow is the worst side of an individual, the part of him/herself he or she either refuses or fails to accept and recognise.

In dreams, the Shadow may appear as a vague, often threatening figure, difficult to discern with clarity. It is invariably antagonistic and usually frightening. Other times it shows up under the guise of an enemy or someone equally detested by the dreamer.

One of the best ways a person can identify some of the contents of his Shadow is by observing his most negative reactions about things and his intense dislike of certain qualities or faults in other people. Those things he abhors so much are the very same things that occupy the core of his Shadow. He must therefore understand this truth about himself because in so doing he will become a better balanced individual.

Anima and Animus

The Anima and the Animus are the concentration of those characteristics of the opposite sex that exist in every human being. The Anima is the hidden female in every man. The Animus, likewise, is the hidden male in every woman.

In a man, the Anima is the centre of the emotional, instinctive and intuitive side of his personality. This archetype is formed of a conglomeration of all the women a man has known in his life, especially his mother. The integration of the Anima will enable a man to develop his sensitive, spontaneous, receptive nature, and allow him to become less aggressive and instead become warmer and more generous and understanding. On the other hand, the repression of his female characteristics will result in obstinacy, hardness, rigidity, and sometimes in irresponsibility and drunkenness.

The Animus in a female acts in a very similar way as the Anima in the male. The ability of a woman to take well-calculated risks, make splitsecond decisions, be strong, level-headed, independent and self-assured, all of these qualities are male characteristics embodied in her

Animus. When a woman ignores this aspect of her nature, she becomes whining, fretful and insecure.

When an individual comes to terms with the Animus or Anima, he or she will have a better understanding of the opposite sex, and will be able to extend the full range and potential of his or her personality.

In dreams, the Anima appears to a man in the figure of a woman with no face, or an unknown face. In a woman's dream, the Animus appears as a group of men or a man with contrasting qualities. Because the Anima and Animus are the result of a transformation of the Shadow, the appearance of either or these two archetypes in dreams may be accompanied by the intrusion of disagreeable unconscious impulses into the conscious personality.

But there is a positive side to this situation. While there will be a period in the individual's life marked by disturbances in normal behaviour patterns, the emergence of the Anima or Animus indicates that the integration of the personality is now under way. This personality integration was called the 'Individuation Process' by Jung.

The Individuation Process
When the Individuation Process is completed, a new and most important archetype emerges from the psyche. This archetype is the Self. At this point, the Anima or Animus, which is the symbol of the unconscious and of all the archetypes, loses it force, releasing great amounts of psychic energy or libido into the psyche. This libido comes to rest in a 'twilight zone' where it acts as a bridge between the conscious and unconscious aspects of the psyche. The harmony that is created when the conflict of opposites expressed by the conscious and the unconscious is resolved is the embodiment of the Self. The Ego of Persona finds itself revolving around the Self, which is now the centre of the psyche and the source of all its energy.

The Higher Self

The Self as an archetype symbolises the higher spiritual aspect of man. It is the Atman, the Higher Self, the Holy Guardian Angel, the Buddha Self, the god within. It is the highest ideal to which man can aspire.

When the Self appears in a dream it usually indicates that the Individuation Process is being completed, and that the personality is being integrated success- fully. In a man's dream, the Self in its totality appears as the Wise Old Man. In a woman's dream, the figure appears as the Great Mother. But in each case, the Self has four main aspects that represent the four qualities of the psyche. These four aspects have both a positive and a negative side, as shown in Table 1.

Table 1

The Great Mother	The Wise Old Man
Intellect	*Intellect*
Amazon (positive)	Hero (positive)
Huntress (negative)	Villain (negative)
Intuition	*Intuition*
Priestess (positive)	Joker (positive)
Evil Witch (negative)	Black Magician (negative)
Emotion	*Emotion*
Princess (positive)	Youth (positive)
Seductress (negative)	Tramp (negative)
Sensation	*Sensation*
Mother (positive)	Father (positive)
Terrible Mother (negative)	Ogre (negative)

The negative aspects of the ideal Self archetype are the remnants of the integrated contents of the Shadow. Whenever they appear in a dream they indicate that their particular forces are being ignored by the individual and that they must be recognised and accepted before full individuation can take place. The Self becomes an integrated whole when all the different aspects are individually developed and absorbed into the personality.

As stated earlier, *the archetypes are part of the Collective Unconscious, and as such they have universal meanings. When one of these archetypes appears in a dream it has similar connotations for all human beings.* The personal parts of a dream are not archetypal in essence, although they can represent aspects of the dreamer's unconscious.

Importance of Jung's Theories
The reason why we have dwelt so extensively in the various psychological schools, and Jung's theories in particular, is that in order to understand the symbology of dreams, and even why we dream at all, we must have a working knowledge of the structure of the human mind or psyche.

Jung's theory of the Collective Unconscious and the archetypes, although often criticised and disparaged, still remains one of the most viable and lucid explanations of the mysteries of the mind. His concept of the libido, the Individuation Process, and his dream theories are all very helpful in the interpretation of dreams, and ultimately in the integration of the personality.

'In difficult cases when I do not know where else to go for help, I try to find it in dreams.'

— *Carl Gustav Jung*

But even Jung himself baulked at the thought of a stereotyped, rigid theory of dream interpretation. He stubbornly reiterated that there was 'no general theory of dreams'. Likewise, there are no fixed meanings for the symbols of the unconscious. It always depends on the dream and specifically on the dreamer. This belief is strongly shared by this author. Therefore, in this guide, although dream interpretation will be conducted along psychological lines, great emphasis will be placed on each individual dreamer and his immediate environment.

2. Why Do We Sleep?

*Death, so called, is a thing which
make men weep,
And yet a third of life is passed
in sleep.*
— Lord Byron, Don Juan, XIV, iii

Every night we go to sleep and, with some rare exceptions, become 'dead to the world' for a period of time that extends on the average to approximately eight hours. Some people spend considerably less time sleeping, while others spend more.

Newborn babies, for example, sleep an average of 17–18 hours a day. Adolescents sleep approximately 10-11 hours in a 24-hour period, while young adults spend an average of eight hours a night sleeping. Elderly people, on the other hand, seldom sleep more than six hours during the night. This seems to indicate that we require less sleep as we grow older, but still, on the whole, we spend approximately one-third of our lives sleeping.

Circadian Rhythms

An immense amount of research is being conducted all over the world on the phenomenon we call sleep. Some amazing discoveries have been made on this, our secret night life, but the most puzzling question still remains essentially unanswered. Why do we grow increasingly dazed every night, until our bodies become clumsy and inoperative, our eyes close unwillingly, and our minds blank out for several hours? This mysterious lethargy that is sleep affects not only human beings but practically every living thing in nature.

Even plants seem to follow a cycle that includes sleep. Some flowers close their petals at night and open them again in the morning, as if they were aware of the transition between night and day. Scientists call these cycles **circadian rhythms**, which are daily fluctuations comprising a 24-hour period. These cycles are presumed to be present in every living cell.

Thus, the whole of nature is engaged in one huge circadian rhythm. Examples of this phenomenon are ocean tides, the setting and rising of the sun, the four seasons, the mating of animals, a woman's ovulating period, and the gestation of mammals.

Sleep is also believed to be controlled by circadian rhythms; that is, we sleep because an internal 'clock' in our brains gives the signal for our bodies to stop their daily activity and go into slumber for a certain amount of time.

This cessation of activity takes place usually at night because our bodies are less functional at this time. Our minds are less receptive to learning, our body temperature lowers, our reflexes are not as quick; in short, we are at low ebb in our mental and physical mechanisms.

Jet Lag

When we alter our sleeping habits, losing several hours or more of sleep, the body reacts with feelings of fatigue, nervousness or irritability. Scientists believe this is due to a 'phase shift' of our circadian rhythm.

Jet lag is a typical example of such a shift. If we fly from California to New York we may have trouble falling

---

'All we see or seem
is but a dream within a dream.'

— *Edgar Allan Poe (1808–49), American writer and poet*

---

asleep the first night because our bodies are still operating on Pacific Time which is three hours earlier than the Eastern Standard Time which operates in New York. And even if we should sleep a full eights hours, we would still find it difficult to awake at eight o'clock the next morning because our internal clocks would tell our bodies it is only five o'clock.

After several days in New York, our bodies would adapt to the change in the time schedule. Upon returning to the West Coast, we would find ourselves three hours ahead of Pacific Time, and again we would need a few days to adjust to the change. A 'phase shift' does not mean, therefore, we have *lost* sleep, but rather that 'body time' is out of phase with 'clock time'.

What Happens When You Don't Sleep?

Actual sleep deprivation, where a person loses more than one night's sleep, does tend to affect the organism, impairing several faculties of the body. After three nights without sleep, the average person complains of itchy eyes and begins to see double. He/she is unable to count past 15, cannot concentrate on any subject for longer than a few minutes, and begins to lose his/her sense of balance. He/she also feels lightheaded and often hears a buzzing sound in his/her ears. In some cases, if the loss of sleep continues, the person begins to develop marked paranoid symptoms.

In 1959, a New York disc jockey named Peter Tripp decided to stay awake for 200 hours in order to raise money for the March of Dimes. During the beginning of the marathon, he was in good spirits and made a daily broadcast from a glass booth in Times Square. But towards the end of the 200 hours, his speech became slurred and incoherent, and soon thereafter his behaviour became pronouncedly paranoid.

These psychotic tendencies made their appearance during the night-time hours, at which time Tripp became convinced that unknown enemies were trying to drug his food in order to force him to fall asleep. This persecution mania was accompanied at times by auditory hallucinations.

Tripp went on to complete his 200-hour sleepless marathon, and soon thereafter recovered from his temporary paranoia. The only treatment he required was a healthy dose of sleep.

The Necessity for Sleep

Since Tripp's experience, many researchers have devoted considerable time and effort to studying the effects of lack of sleep in the human body, and specifically, in the human mind. With some rare exceptions, they have discovered that sleep deprivation is detrimental to the perfect internal harmony of man. Even animals show negative effects in the absence of sleep, and baby animals, such as kittens, will die if they are not allowed to sleep for several days.

Those people who allegedly feel no ill effects in the absence of sleep are probably unaware of the existence of short sleep periods known as microsleep. This means that a person may doze off for a few seconds without realising it. These short sleep periods may then repeat themselves intermittently throughout the night, providing the individual with enough sleep to function normally.

Why We Need Sleep

So we know that pronounced loss of sleep is detrimental to the body and the mind. In other words, we *need* sleep. The question is *why*.

Experiments by NASA have shown that the relief of body fatigue is not the specific function of sleep. We do not sleep only to rest. On the other hand, Navy studies have proven that prolonged isolation decreases the need

for sleep in an individual. This would seem to indicate that less interaction with other people and less outside stimuli would result in a need for less sleep.

Sleep control centres are located in the brain stem, which is an area the size of one's little finger at the base of the brain. Scientists believe the brain stem contains a system whose activity ensures wakefulness in the individual, while its inactivity leads to sleep.

Russian Nobel Laureate Ivan Pavlov, who was a neurophysiologist, believed the brain's natural state is wakefulness. In other words, the brain is always awake and active, and its activity is only interrupted for the restoration and recovery of the body.

During sleep, the body is functioning only at a very low level, stressing the important role played by the brain in keeping it awake. This role is dramatically emphasised in sleep disorders such an apnoea, where a person cannot breathe while asleep, and narcolepsy, where a person will fall asleep every few minutes, regardless of the time and place he may find himself. People afflicted with these tragic diseases can never hope to lead a completely normal life, at least until science can find both the reason and cure for these disorders.

If Pavlov's theory is correct, as many scientists seem to believe, and the brain's natural state is wakefulness, and if rest is not the specific function of sleep, why sleep at all, especially considering that the body is functioning at a lesser level during sleep?

Nature is immensely logical and prosaic in its evolutionary processes. It seldom commits blunders, and when it does, they are seldom of major importance. Therefore, the evolution of such a complex organism as man, with a thoroughly wasteful timing device such as unnecessary sleep worked in, seems inconceivable.

The act of falling asleep is the result of lying down and relaxing the body. After some time has elapsed, the heart and respiration rate will decrease, blood pressure will be lowered, and body temperature will drop below its normal level. If the individual continues to lie still without moving, he will eventually fall asleep. But he will never know exactly when because even with the help of an electroencephalogram it is impossible to determine the exact moment a person falls asleep.

What typifies the onset of sleep is the loss of awareness. We fall asleep at the exact moment an external stimulus, such as a noise, fails to evoke a response in us.

REM and NREM

Scientists have discovered that there are two types of sleep. These have been called REM (Rapid Eye Movement) and NREM, pronounced 'non-REM'.

The NREM state is the first sleep period of the night. It is often called the 'quiet sleep' because it is characterised by slow, regular breathing, an absence of body movements, and decreased brain activity. The sleeper has simply lost contact with his/her environment due to his/her brain's lethargy. He/she is no longer receiving information through his/her five senses and, therefore, he/she is not reacting to his/her surroundings. The body is able to move during this stage but it does not because the brain does not tell it to do so.

There are several NREM periods during the night. The first one lasts approximately 80 minutes. It is immediately followed by the first REM period, which usually lasts about ten minutes.

The REM period is characterised by small, convulsive twitches of the hands and facial muscles. If the individual has been snoring, he/she stops, and his/her breathing becomes irregular and laboured. His/her body becomes completely paralysed, and he/she is unable to move his/her arms, legs or trunk. Blood pressure usually soars during this period and the heart beat increases as if the sleeper were running an obstacle course. Most significantly, the eyes begin to move rapidly from side to side under the closed eyelids, as if the sleeper were looking at a moving object.

Saint Thomas Aquinas (1225–74), Italian theologian and philosopher, believed in the prophetic character of dreams both as a reaction to things to come and as a causal factor in future events.

I (dreamed I) was in Bonaparte's palace, where some sort of a contest was taking place between him and Sir Sidney Smith, who came to me for a knife to cut something which prevented him from drawing his sword. Bonaparte struck me; I had an axe in my hand; he saw that I was half inclined to cut him down, and attempted to kill me. I struck him with the axe, and brought him down, and I dragged him out into a public hall, not being yet dead, and there beheaded him. This is the first time I ever killed him in self-defence, though I have more than once done it upon the pure principle of tyrannicide.

— *Robert Southey (1774–1843), English poet*

Researchers have discovered that if a person within the REM stage is awakened he/she will invariably say that he/she has been dreaming. Thus, the REM sleep period has been identified with the dreaming state in the human being, although the same phenomenon has been noticed in animals, leading scientists to think that humans may not be the only ones to dream.

All during the night the NREM and the REM stages of sleep alternate with each other. The cycle varies from 70 to 110 minutes, but the average is 90 minutes.

In the beginning of sleep, the NREM periods are longer, but as the night progresses, REM periods grow longer, at times lasting for as long as one hour. Thus, in general, we can say that we dream approximately every 90 minutes throughout the night, and that we dream roughly two hours out of every eight-hour sleep.

Need for REM Sleep

Advanced sleep research has uncovered the fact that REM sleep is needed by the human being. Individuals who have volunteered to sleep and be observed in sleep laboratories have reacted very negatively when they have not been allowed to complete any of their REM periods. They became nervous, irritable, and erratic in their behaviour, and slept badly and uncomfortably.

So, the general conclusion has been that *sleep is necessary, particularly the portion of sleep that is connected with dreaming. Many scientists believe the THE ONLY REASON WHY WE SLEEP IS SO THAT WE MAY DREAM.*

Babies, who sleep between 16 and 18 hours a day, spend more than 50 per cent of this time in the REM stage. Does this mean that babies are dreaming all during this time? If so, what about? *Could their unconscious minds be releasing from the Collective Unconscious enough stored information to prepare each baby for his/her new life?*

And what about the rest of us? Why do we dream?

Could it be that we dream so that our unconscious minds may unravel and absorb the problems and happenings of each day, incorporating them into the neat filing system of the Collective Unconscious?

Maybe a dream is the way the unconscious mind copes with things, helping the individual interact satisfactorily with his/her environment. In other words, perhaps at least some dreams bring to bear on the individual dreamer's problems and needs the resources of the Collective Unconscious – the total, cumulative experience of Humanity that we all share in at this level!

For that reason, sleep deprivation, particularly REM sleep, is detrimental to the individual's health and well-being. Significantly, one of the first indications of mental illness is a marked disturbance in the person's sleeping patterns.

But what is a dream? What causes it and how is it produced? Most importantly, what does it mean to us in our waking lives?

3. What Is a Dream?

All this we see or seem
is but a dream within a dream
– Edgar Allan Poe, A Dream Within a Dream

During Freud's time, dreams were believed to be the 'guardians of sleep'. One dreamt in order not to wake up. Whenever a disturbance arose in the vicinity of a sleeper, the brain manufactured a dream that would prevent the individual from being awakened.

Freud himself felt that dreams were interwoven around the noise or outside stimulus to form a story that would safeguard the person's sleep.

For many years this theory persisted, even after the discovery of REM sleep. A dripping tap, the sound of a siren or an alarm clock, the need to urinate, or a full stomach were all considered the prime suspects in the causation of dreams, and even in the onset of REM sleep itself.

But eventually this theory was disproven because it has been shown in laboratory experiments that the REM period, and thus dreaming, is determined by a biochemical process which is circadian (cyclic) in nature, and *not* caused by outside influences.

*A dream can incorporate a disturbing stimulus into its plot, but it cannot be **initiated** by this stimulus. In other words, dreams are not instantaneous occurrences, but very well-planned ones.*

The Stuff Dreams Are Made Of
The dream experience can vary widely between individual

dreamers. To some, the actions in a dream follow logical sequences, while to others, dreams are irrational and illogical.

Some people have symbolic, abstract dreams, while others have realistic dreams as normal as waking life.

Some dreams can seem intensely real, while others are so fantastic that we become aware that we must be dreaming.

Dreams can be alternately dull and exciting, creative and destructive, frightening and enjoyable.

Some fulfill our wishes, others frustrate them.

A dream can depress us to the point of tears or fill us with hope and inspiration. Sometimes they seem to control us, and sometimes we control them.

Some people can dream at will, and some can return to a dream they started the night before.

But whatever the 'stuff dreams are made of', the important thing is they seem to be real to the brain.

Jung believed that the unconscious mind is the 'matrix' of dreams, and that therefore dreams were the exponents of the human psyche. He also believed that dreams provide the bulk of the material necessary for the proper investigation of the psyche, and that dream interpretation on a large scale would, after some time, surrender the complete programming of an individual's mind.

Contrary to Freud, Jung believed that outside organic sensations did not cause a dream. This view was to be confirmed many years later in sleep laboratories, as we have seen. Instead, Jung felt that dreams are the remnants of a 'peculiar psychic activity' taking place during a sleep.

'The dream is its own interpretation.'

– from the Talmud, the compilation of ancient Jewish law

Freud's Dream Theories

Nevertheless, Freud's theories on dreams laid the ground-work for much of the research that was to be conducted on the subject by other workers, including Jung. Some of Freud's ideas have been disproved, but others remain at the core of modern dream theories.

Central to Freud's theory of dreams was his wish-fulfilment theory. According to Freud, dreams are essentially the result of repressed wishes that come to the surface of our consciousness when we are asleep. These wishes, unacceptable to the conscious personality, are satisfied and fulfilled during dreams, but in symbolic form only. So well-disguised are these repressed desires that we are unable for the most part to identify them when we awake.

The mental agency responsible for the distortion of dream images was named first the Censor by Freud, and then the Superego. The idea behind the distorted dream is to keep the sleeper from waking up, by expressing the repressed wish in veiled terms.

Freud believed that the mind works in two totally opposite ways. The first type, which he called the Primary Process, is characterised by symbolisation, ignorance of the concepts of time and space, and wish-fulfilling hallucinations.

The second type, known as the Secondary Process, is governed by reason and logic, observance of time and space, and learned adaptive behaviour.

The Primary Process is exemplified by the state of dreaming and the Secondary Process by conscious thinking.

Freud believed the dream state or Primary Process preceded the conscious state or Secondary Process, and that the latter, as well as all ego development and the acquisition of a thinking apparatus, depends largely on the repression of the dreams and hallucinations which are part of the Primary Process. In other words, we dream before we think. This theory was Freud's major contribution to the understanding of dreams.

Also according to Freud, a dream has two sets of 'contents'. One of these sets, the *latent* content, is the true message of the dream, what the unconscious is trying to say to the conscious personality.

The second set is known as the *manifest* content and it represents the actual dream remembered by the dreamer. In other words, the latent content of the dream is translated into the symbolic imagery which is known as the manifest content. Again, the purpose of these masquerades is to prevent the sleeper from waking up.

Freud's Dream Analysis Method

The best way, according to Freud, that one can decipher the convoluted symbolism of dreams, is by discovering the first idea that occurs to the dreamer when he thinks of his dream, and then following it to see where it leads, or where it meets with a mental block.

The idea behind this theory is that all the associations with the various details of the dream will eventually disclose a recurrent theme, which will be the message of the unconscious, or the latent content of the dream. This system of dream elucidation was called by Freud **free association**.

Jung also used free association in his dream interpretations, but he did not share Freud's belief that *all* dreams are the result of wish-fulfilment. He felt some wish-fulfilment is present in some dreams, but not in all.

Jung's Dream Theories

To Jung, our lives are spent in the midst of struggles in order to realise our wishes. If we cannot fulfill these wishes in reality, then we do it in a fantasy, in a dream. The use of free association comes in when we try to discover the

'Dreams are absolutely egoistic.'

— *Sigmund Freud (1856–1939), Austrian father of psychoanalysis*

experience or experiences that caused this dream or fantasy. Jung called this use of free association, **amplification**.

Some people feel that it seems useless to have dreams if we cannot understand them. But this, strangely enough, is not true. We can reap benefits from a dream whether we understand it or not. This is because the unconscious uses a different type of language than that of the conscious mind, and it also offers a totally different point of view. This amounts to a psychological adjustment, a 'compensation' which is absolutely necessary for a proper balance between conscious and unconscious actions.

When we are awake, we reflect on every problem with the utmost care. But often we go to sleep with our unsolved problems very much present in our minds. The unconscious mind continues our exploration of the problem on a deeper level. It is able to grasp aspects of our problems we either ignored or were unaware of. Through dream symbology the unconscious helps us to cope with our problems, even in those instances when the problems cannot be immediately solved.

We awaken from the dream with a sense of balance, with the feeling that we can and will overcome our problems. That is the reason some people like to 'sleep' on a problem, while everyone feels 'like new' after a good night's rest. We simply dream our cares away.

Listening to Our Dreams
While it is true that we do not have to understand our dreams to benefit from them, it is also true we can enhance

their effect considerably if we try to understand them. This is often necessary because 'the voice of the unconscious' is easily ignored and seldom heard.

In order for us to understand the voice of the unconscious, we have to become familiar with the language it speaks. This language, as we have seen, is largely symbolical. The symbolism of dreams can be interpreted through either *a causal* or *a final* standpoint.

Dream Symbolism

The causal standpoint, which was used by Freud, starts from a desire or craving – that is, from a depressed dream-wish. This craving is always something comparatively simple, which can hide itself in a great variety of ways.

For instance, a repressed sexual impulse can be expressed in a dream as putting a key in a lock to open a door, flying through the air, or dancing.

To the typical Freudian, all oblong objects in a dream are phallic symbols, while round or hollow objects are feminine symbols.

In other words, the causal standpoint gives a fixed meaning to each symbol in a dream, regardless of who is the dreamer.

Specific Individual Symbolism

The final standpoint gives each image a specific meaning. These meanings vary, not only between individual dreamers but also between different dreams. In this system, dreaming of opening a door means an entirely different thing from dreaming of flying through the air.

Which of these two standpoints do we use in interpreting a dream? According to Jung, we should use both.

The causal standpoint provides the fixed meaning that has been given to a specific symbol by the collective unconscious. This means that every symbol has a fixed meaning for every human being.

The final standpoint gives a second meaning to the same symbol, namely that which the dreamer associates with that particular image. This is the personalised aspect of a dream, and that which makes it individual.

Jung held the interesting idea that the abstract and figurative language of dreams, which is reminiscent of the Biblical use of parables and of the symbolism of primitive languages, could well be the survival of an archaic mode of thought used by man in prehistoric times.

Dreams are often in opposition to our conscious plan. This is not always very marked. Sometimes it is a subtle deviation from the conscious attitude, but occasionally it coincides with the conscious plans. This behaviour of the dream is called **compensation** by Jung, and it means a balancing and compounding of different data and points of view in order to produce adjustment and rectification between the conscious and the unconscious aspects of the personality.

Dream Interpretation

Although the conscious attitude of a person may be known, the attitude of the unconscious is not. This can be learned through dream interpretation.

When the conscious and the unconscious are unbalanced, this can be very dangerous for the individual, as the unconscious is very capable of destroying the personality if left to its own devices. The correct interpretation and understanding of dreams can help reveal any dangerous rifts between the conscious and the unconscious, in time to effect the proper harmony between the two.

Jung identified several types of dreams. The **compensatory** dream, which has just been described, adds to the conscious mind all those elements from the previous day which remained ignored either because of repression or because they were too weak to reach consciousness. In a sense, this dream acts as a self-regulation of the psyche.

Dreams of Prediction

The **prospective** dream is an anticipation of future conscious achievements or happenings, a form of advance blueprint of the individual's life. Its symbolic contents may outline the upcoming solution of a conflict or prepare the dreamer for a distressing future occurrence.

Although the prospective dream is often called prophetic, Jung tells us that in the vast majority of cases they are merely an anticipatory combination of probabilities that may coincide with the actual development of things.

This is not surprising because a dream is the result of the fusion of repressed elements and is therefore a combination of all the feelings, thoughts and ideas that have not been registered by the consciousness. In other words, *dreams know things we do not and are, therefore, in a better position than we are to predict the outcome of many things.*

Telepathic Dreams

Although he felt that the majority of prophetic dreams were prospective and naturally explainable, Jung also believed that there are some dreams that are decidedly telepathic and that no amount of learned dissertation can change that truth. Some people seem to have this ability and often have telepathically influenced dreams.

Jung did not attempt to offer a theory for this phenomenon, but he believed that most telepathic dreams are affected by a powerful human emotion, such as love or grief. Thus, most telepathic dreams predict the arrival

---

Our dreams are tales
Told in dim Eden
By Eve's nightingales

     – Walter De La Mare (1873–1956), English poet and novelist

---

or the death of a loved one, or any happening that will deeply affect the dreamer.

Nightmares

The **nightmare**, which haunts so many of man's dreams, is a compensatory dream of vital significance for the consciousness because it often warns the individual his conscious actions are threatening his/her well-being.

We invariably have nightmares if we overeat or otherwise overindulge our senses. We also have 'bad dreams' when we are doing something reprehensible or socially unacceptable. It is our unconscious way of saying we are endangering our physical or mental balance. If we persist in our negative actions, the nightmares may get worse, and the unconscious will find a way of either correcting our behaviour or destroying our personality and us.

Other Disturbing Dreams

Reductive, or negative, dreams are dreams that bring the dreamer down a notch or two. The people who have these dreams have an unusually high opinion of themselves and are constantly impressing it on others. The unconscious mind, who knows perfectly well there is a lot of hot air in these balloons, perversely sets out to burst them in a colourful explosion of horrid imagery.

Jung used to recall with great gusto the dreams of one of his patients, a pedantic aristocrat who held herself in great esteem, but who would go to sleep at night only to dream of dirty fishwives and drunken prostitutes.

Reaction dreams reproduce experiences we have had. These are often caused by traumatic experiences and will repeat themselves until the traumatic stimulus is exhausted. When the reaction dream is recognised through dream interpretation, it usually stops recurring.

Recurrent dreams are particularly present in youth,

'I've dreamt in my life dreams that have stayed with me ever after, and changed my ideas; they've gone through and through me like wine through water, and altered the colour of my mind.'

— *Emily Brontë, author of Wuthering Heights*

although they can also make their appearance in later years. The recurrent dream can be very disturbing because it invariably leaves us with the impression that it must have a special meaning. We feel haunted by the recurrent dream.

The feeling, according to Jung, is invariably correct because this type of dream is usually caused by a psychic disturbance. The identification of the latent content of this dream usually marks the end of its occurrence.

The Uncommon Dream
Most dreams, however, can be more simply divided into two groups, namely, the 'little' dreams and the 'big' dreams. The little dreams are very common, and are mostly of the compensatory type. They are easy to identify because they are equally easy to forget.

The big dreams, on the other hand, are never forgotten. They often contain symbolic images of an archetypal or mythological nature. Godlike figures, princes, castles, dragons, snakes, lightning bolts, the Wise Old Man, Christ are typical of this type of dream. These figures come from the collective unconscious and usually have an important message for the dreamer.

These dreams occur in critical phases of life, and we have all had at least one of these dreams. It is the kind of dream that makes us say 'I will not forget that dream as long as I live'. And we usually don't.

Common Symbols
There are some symbols that recur in everyone's dreams.

God turn to good now all our dreams
For one great mystery, to me it seems,
Is how it is that dreams are born
Whether at evening or at morn,
And why it is that some come true,
While others never ever do.
Why that's a dream of things to come,
Why this a revelation,
Why this a nightmare, that a dreaming,
Never holding for all men the same meaning,
Why this is an apparition, why these are oracles,
I know not, but if the causes of these miracles
Are known by someone better than I
Let him explain them…

— *from The House of Fame by Geoffrey Chaucer (?1340–1400)*

Typical among these are dreams of flying, of climbing stairs or mountains, of falling, of hotels, of trains, of weddings and of being naked.

These symbols are known as **dream motifs** and give some support to the theory that there is a fixed meaning to dream symbols. These motifs become particularly significant in a series of dreams of a recurrent nature.

Dream Interpretation

But how about the method to interpret this great variety of dreams? Jung did not offer a simple system for dream interpretation, but he had several important suggestions.

1. One of these is to make sure that every shade of meaning which each detail of the dream has for the dreamer is determined by the associations of the dreamer him/herself. This means that every individual who wishes to decipher his/her own dreams should attempt to find meanings to each detail of his/her dreams by

writing down the first thing that comes to his/her mind in connection with that particular motif. This should be followed through with as long a list of associations as possible for each symbol. This should reveal to the individual what personal meaning each symbol has for him/her. This procedure was called by Jung 'taking up the context'.

2. The causal, or fixed, meaning of each symbol should also be taken into consideration, and a dictionary of dreams can be useful for this purpose, as it gives the accepted traditional meanings of dreams.

3. Lastly, and perhaps the most interesting of Jung's suggestions, is that one should turn to the past and reconstruct former experiences from the occurrence of certain symbols in his dreams. This should tell us what type of happening we can expect after dreaming with a certain motif.

If we combine these three methods, we should be able to intepret our dreams with relative ease. In the process, we would be learning much about our unconscious attitudes and would be creating a greater harmony between the conscious and the unconscious aspects of our personalities.

'To sleep, perchance to dream: ay, there's the rub.'
— *Hamlet, Act III, Scene I*

---

4. The Symbology of Dreams

For 'tis not doubtable, but that
the mind is working, in the dullest
depth of sleep.
– Owen Felltham, Of Dreams, c. 1620

We already said that there are two sets of meanings to every dream, the **latent** and the **manifest**. The **latent** meaning is the true message that the unconscious is trying to convey to the conscious personality. As this message emerges from the depths of the unconscious mind, it becomes translated into symbolic imagery which is then presented to the consciousness in dream form. This imagery comprises the **manifest** meaning of the dream.

Why Do We Dream in Symbols?
Why does the unconscious use symbols to convey messages to the conscious personality? Freud believed the reason for this need of disguising the true message was to prevent the sleeper from waking up. This explanation does not satisfy many psychologists and dream experts, who believe that the reason we dream in symbols is that symbology is the language of the unconscious.

In other words, we think and even feel in symbols. The reason for this phenomenon is that we are constantly bombarded by visual images during our waking periods. Many of these images are registered by our eyes and by our unconscious minds, but not by our conscious awareness.

Again, many of these images, even the ones we consciously acknowledge, are not accompanied by either sounds or explanations for their existence. They are simply recorded and stored in our mental depths and quickly forgotten by our conscious minds. Many of these images resurface during our dreams in connection with any specific problem or thought we had at the same time we saw that particular thing. To our unconscious mind that visual image became a symbol of the problem or thought we were entertaining at the time. It is interesting to note in this context that blind people have dreams that are totally lacking in visual imagery.

From the preceding it is easy to understand why most psychologists have concluded that many of the symbols that appear in dreams are directly related to visual images which have been seen by the dreamer at one time or another, most often during the previous day. This would tend to make the interpretation of dreams rather difficult without a knowledge of the circumstances surrounding each individual dreamer.

However, there is still another set of symbols that reoccur in everyone's dreams, regardless of the images we see during the day. These are the symbols Jung called dream **motifs**, and which tend to support the theory that there is a fixed meaning to some of the symbology that is part of the deep unconscious.

As we said earlier, some of the most typical dream motifs are dreams of falling, of flying, of climbing stairs or mountains and of riding in trains, buses or automobiles. Dreams with death or with the dead, as well as dreams of weddings, of teeth, of ships, or nakedness and swimming or drowning are also common.

We all have dreamt about all or almost all of these motifs, and in practically all cases the meanings seem to be the same. Of course, we must always analyse each dream in the context of each dreamer's private life. But dream motifs as such seem to share the same meaning in all members of civilised societies. This would tend to place these particular symbols within the realm of the collective unconscious, which, as we have seen, is the common working ground for all human minds. Dream motifs are the subject of all dream dictionaries, including the one presented here.

Colours and Numbers in Dreams

Strangely enough, although our waking life is vibrant with rich colours, not all our dreams have colours in them. It is true that some people seem to dream in colour all the time, but they are in a small minority, because it has been ascertained by several competent researchers that most people have more dreams in black and white than in bright technicolor. Actually, the term 'black and white' is misleading because colourless dreams seldom show a distinction between any hues. They are rather drab in tone and the hues seem to belong to the dullest ranges of grey and brown.

Calvin Hall, perhaps the greatest modern authority on dreams, collected thousands of dreams during his research studies, and was able to report eventually that only 29 per cent of the recorded dreams had been in colour.

As to the most common colours which appear in dreams, Dr Fred Snyder, a pioneer in dream studies, found that the most recurrent colour in dreams was green, with red following close behind. Yellow and blue were only half as common as green.

Dr Patricia Garfield, another dream researcher, made a special analysis of her own dreams and discovered that colour appeared more often in her dreams after several hours of rest. Dr Garfield concluded that there may be a common chemical base for the occurrence of colours in dreams and that perhaps the cerebral cortex is more aroused when the body has been at rest for some time.

'There is no law to judge of the lawless, or canon by which a dream may be criticised.'

Charles Lamb (1775–1834), essayist and critic

Cayce's Colour Theory

Edgar Cayce, the famed 'sleeping prophet', believed that sometimes colour in a dream is used to underline certain conditions in our lives in order to heighten our awareness. To Cayce, bright, clear colours were indicative of positive aspects or trends in our lives, while muddy, drab colours had negative associations. A combination of green and blue in a peaceful setting could be an indication of healing of mind or body, while deep greys or dark browns could show a pessimistic outlook for any given situation surrounding the dream.

According to Cayce, personal likes and dislikes in colours affect their meaning in dreams. For example, if you prefer green over any other colour and you have a dream where green is the most predominant colour, this would mean that your unconscious is giving you an optimistic message about the particular situation depicted in the dream. On the other hand, if you loathe the colour green, to see it in a dream would indicate you have deep negative feelings about the subject of your dream.

Meanings of Colour

In general, colours in dreams have been ascribed meaning as shown in the following Dictionary pp. 96–7.

Naturally, the type of object we see surrounded by a specific colour in a dream is just as important as its hue, and we have to take both meanings into consideration before reaching a reasonably accurate interpretation of the dream.

Scientists have proved that endocrine therapy with pituitary extract produced vivid, brightly coloured, pleasant dreams full of hope and elation. Morphine produced coloured dreams. Under nitrous oxide (laughing gas), the concept of ego in dreams was weakened. In addition, it has been proved that external stimuli: tickling, the placing of a close-fitting mask on the sleeper's face, strong odours and heat were able to produce respondent dreams.

Other scientists have claimed that they can induce 'lucid dreams', that is the dream the sleeper desires, through a variety of means.

Number Symbology

Numbers are also important in dream interpretation, and they have been the subject of extensive research on the part of psychologists.

To Jung, for example, numbers predated man and in fact had been discovered rather than invented by human kind. Jung went one step further and stated that 'it would not be such an audacious conclusion after all if we define number psychologically as the archetype of order which has become conscious.' This means that the unconscious uses numbers as 'ordering factors', that is, as a means of creating order in the universe. In other words, *each number has a specific meaning for the unconscious mind, a meaning that is the same for each individual member of the human race.*

Some ancient languages were structured upon the same belief. The Hebrew language, for example, still in use, uses the same characters for both letters and numbers. Each Hebrew letter and therefore each number, represents a cosmic state and has a specific meaning.

In modern times, each number from 0 to 9 has also been ascribed a special meaning. When the number is larger than 9, its digits are added until the number is reduced to one digit, not larger than 9. This is done because there are only ten pure ciphers, each one indicating a state of mind. These ciphers extend from 0 to 9. When a composite number seems very significant, instead of reducing the number to one digit, it is far more enlightening to look at each of the individual ciphers that compose the number and find each of their meanings. One can then apply these meanings to the problem presented in the dream, and find an inner guidance to its possible solution.

However, there is another instance when the larger composite numbers should not be reduced to a single digit, or even analysed in terms of the individual ciphers. If such a number appears as significant in a 'big' dream, then it will have a symbolical meaning all its own – a meaning that may be revealed in an intuitive flash, through meditation, or through an understanding of **gematria**.

Gematria, part of the ancient Hebrew Kabbalah, recognises certain numbers as having *archetypal* meanings that can be explored through established 'correspondences', or associations of words having similar numerical values. *See Dictionary pp. 143–4.*

If a native of Kamchatka in the eastern part of the Soviet Union dreams that he possesses something that belongs to another and tells him of the dream, the other person says: 'Take it; it is mine no longer.' He would fear that his life would be in danger if he did not obey the injunction of the other's dream.

Gambler's Numbers

There is another set of meanings attributed to dreams and numbers which has come down to us through many diverse traditions. These are the numbers that are popularly used for betting and gambling purposes. In these cases, each dream motif has also been ascribed a special number. No one knows for sure the origins of this custom, but many professional gamblers scan their dreams carefully in search of clues to winning numbers.

Time and Space

Often in dreams the symbology with which we are faced fails to indicate whether we are observing a past, present or future event. This happens because the human unconscious moves in a space-time continuum where past, present and future exist simultaneously along various points of space. This means that the unconscious mind does not differentiate between time spans, and therefore does not make any effort to distinguish between the past and the future, the present and the past, or the present and the future.

Nevertheless, because time moves in space, we can ascertain time in dreams if we observe the position of objects in a dream. For instance, approaching objects usually denote the future and receding objects, the past. An immovable object usually represents the present. Some psychologists believe that objects on the right side of the dream 'picture' tend to relate to the future and those on the left, to the past. The possible solution to a problem is sometimes indicated by a door, a lift or a crossroads.

Do Dreams Foretell the Future?

But can a dream truly foretell the future? The answer is yes, according to the innumerable case histories recorded by dream researchers.

This phenomenon, which Jung called the **prospective** dream, can be explained through the ability of the unconscious mind to bring to the surface of the consciousness events from the future. In other words, the unconscious

---

A prayer to Shamaz, Babylonian sun-god and 'Lord of Visions':
'Reveal thyself unto me and let me see a favourable dream,
May the dream that I dream be favourable,
May the dream that I dream be true,
May Mamú, the Goddess of dreams, stand at my head
Let me enter E-Sagila, the temple of the gods, the house of life.'

To know whom you shall marry, this is what you have to do, according to the seventeenth-century antiquarian and author, John Aubrey:

You must lie in another county, and knit the left garter about the right legged stocking (let the other garter and stocking alone) and as you rehearse these following verses, at every comma, knit a knot:

> 'This knot I knit,
> To know the thing, I know not yet
> That I may see,
> The man (woman) that shall my husband (wife) be,
> How he goes, and what he wears,
> And what he does, all days and years.'

Accordingly in your dream you will see him: if a musician, with a lute or other instrument; if a scholar, with book and papers.

mind seems to know what is going to happen, and this knowledge extends infinitely in time. The knowledge of future events can be made known to us through dreams, as well as through telepathy, clairvoyance or clairaudience.

Jung explained this extraordinary power of the unconscious mind as the principle of **synchronicity**. According to Jung, many circumstances in a person's life that are dismissed as 'coincidences', are in reality *meaningful* in the sense that they are messages from the unconscious mind.

Examples of this type of coincidence are the telephone call or the letter from a person about whom we were just thinking; the 'hunch' that turned out to be correct; the dream that foretold an event that took place a few days later. Not coincidences, said Jung, but examples of synchronicity, or the harmonious working of all human minds within the conglomerate which is the collective unconscious.

Sex in Dreams

Sex is sometimes explicit and other times implicit in our dreams. This means that some of our dreams are openly

For life is but a Dream whose shapes return
Some frequently, some seldom, some by night and
Some by day

B.V. Thompson (1834–1882), English poet

concerned with sex, and others use symbols to denote sexual activity.

Notable among sexual symbols in dreams are very physical activities such as dancing, flying through the air or riding a horse. Always take special note of the individual with whom you dance in a dream, for that person is assuredly a very desirable sexual playmate to you either consciously or unconsciously.

It is important also to note that person's attitude towards you in the dream, for that is also a message from your unconscious to you. If the person seems uninterested or unwilling to dance with you, chances are you are wasting your time entertaining any amorous thoughts towards him or her. On the other hand, if your dancing partner seems eager and pleased to be in your company, you can be sure that person will be very receptive to any sexual advances on your part.

Open sexuality in dreams usually denotes sexual repression in the dreamer's daily life. These dreams are often 'wish fulfilments', and should be treated as such. Sometimes people become very concerned with dreams of abnormal sexual activity, such as homosexual encounters or plain exhibitionism.

Most psychologists advise against taking this type of dream seriously, as it may often express an aspect of the dreamer's own self. Making love to a person of one's own sex could be simply an expression of self-love, a message from the unconscious that we should take better care of the self. A exhibitionist dream could indicate a need to be more open to others.

The sexual dream should be interpreted in the same manner as any other type of dream – the unconscious' message duly noted and heeded, and then the dream dismissed. It is unwise to worry over this or any other type of dream, for any excessive concern about any given subject tends to affect the delicate balance of the human mind.

The Dream's Purpose

What the dream and its symbology is doing is helping us to 'digest' the problems and occurrences of our daily lives. By means of dreams, the unconscious helps us to adapt to each day's changes and the challenges we are continuously facing. When a dream is threatening, the unconscious is telling us that there is a situation around us, depicted in the dream, which is out of control, and which we should try to overcome. Invariably within that same dream's symbology, we can find the solution to that particular problem.

Our personal problems, our fears, our likes and dislikes, our hopes, and our needs, all of these are reflected in symbolic form in our dreams. That is why we must take into consideration all the circumstances that surround us when we interpret a dream.

The purpose of dream interpretation is to try to understand the language of the unconscious mind and to listen to its suggestions and explanations. This is of vital importance because when we understand the message from the unconscious mind, we also understand what makes us 'tick', and are in a better position to control and direct our lives.

5. The Nightmare

Her lips were red, her looks were free,
Her locks were yellow as gold:
Her skin was white as leprosy,
The Nightmare Life-in-Death was she,
Who thicks man's blood with cold.
– Coleridge, The Ancient Mariner, III

We are all familiar with the nightmare. We have all experienced the pounding heart, the sweating body, the laboured breathing, the feeling of horror and impending disaster which are associated with this nighttime terror. But what causes the nightmare? Why does the human unconscious release a poisonous stream of terrifying images at certain given times during our sleep?

Overeating and the Nightmare

Some scientists advise against going to sleep immediately after a large meal because they believe a full stomach can be the culprit in a great deal of nightmares. We all know Dagwood of the famed *Blondie* cartoons and his weakness for monster-sized sandwiches. The consumption of these stratospheric concoctions was invariably followed by a monster-sized nightmare, well-seasoned with a few monsters of its own. In keeping with the old adage, we can say that many a truth is said in jest, and this is also the case in Dagwood Bumstead's nightmares.

The reason why overeating can lead to nightmares is twofold. First of all, there is usually a feeling of guilt connected with overeating. This guilt is reflected in the punitive actions of the terrifying characters of the nightmare. They chase, threaten, attack, and generally bully the dreamer into a state of nervous collapse. These self-inflicted terrors seem almost designed to deter the dreamer from overeating again before going to sleep.

The second aspect of this situation to be considered is the fact that the monsters and threatening figures in the nightmare are images released by an overactive brain working double time to process digestion and keep watch over the body as the individual rests. A great many chemical substances are at work in the body at this time, and the increased activity of both brain and heart, which should naturally be working less during sleep, tends to bring out the most negative images stored in the unconscious. It is almost as if the unconscious mind were getting even with the conscious aspect of the personality for making it work at a time when it should be able to relax.

Drug Abuse and the Nightmare

But overeating is not the only cause of the nightmare. Drug abuse, as well as sudden drug withdrawal, can also result in the most nerve-shattering nightmares.

Dr William C. Dement, a world-famous authority on sleep and dream phenomena, has determined that sleeping pills can cause what he calls 'profoundly disturbed sleep'. Dr Dement says that many people who start taking sleeping pills to alleviate their insomnia find after some time that they need increasingly large doses of the medication for it to be effective. Eventually their dependence on the sleeping pills is so great that they can no longer sleep without them. Whenever they attempt to sleep without medication they either cannot sleep at all or else they sleep only to be tormented by terrifying nightmares.

Dr Anthony Kale, who does sleep research at the Pennsylvania State University Medical School, has confirmed Dr Dement's findings on the sleep disturbances connected with drug abuse and drug withdrawal.

Recurrent or continuous nightmares are so disruptive of the normal thought patterns of the mind that they are considered by psychiatrists to be one of the first symptoms of an impending nervous breakdown. This does not mean that every bad dream should be seen as the precursor of mental collapse, but recurrent or persistent nightmares, accompanied by other sleep disturbances, should be promptly consulted with the family physician or with a competent psychologist or psychiatrist.

Other Causes

But what causes the recurrent nightmare or any nightmare that is not sparked by overeating or drugs?

Dr Dement thinks that the intensity of brain stem activity and the activation of 'primitive' emotional circuits may be what determines the sense of dread in dreams. These primitive circuits are naturally buried in the depths of the unconscious mind and are, therefore, not only difficult to control, but also largely responsible for the release of the most horrible images within the unconscious.

Fear is one of the most primitive urges in the human being, and the things we fear the most, we try to avoid by burying them deep within the unconscious mind. Any sympathetic emotion, such as fear itself, worry, anxiety or insecurity over any given situation, can trigger the hidden mechanisms that activate what Dr Dement calls the 'primitive emotional circuits', causing the flow of the negative imagery we call the nightmare.

Death Symbols in Dreams

Jung, on the other hand, noted that actual death is often announced by symbols that indicate changes, rebirth of journeys. Long trips by train, ship or airplane are particularly suspicious, but only if they repeat themselves constantly over a period of a year.

The same holds true for dreams of moving from one place to another, coming out of deep water, or drowning in it. This latter dream can also indicate the danger of mental illness, as deep water usually symbolises the unconscious mind.

But again, these findings are not conclusive because these same dreams can simply mean not death but a new growth and transformation of the personality, as it occurs when the individuation process is completed.

What to Do About the Nightmares

What all of this means is that we cannot offer a perfectly valid or clear explanation of the causes of the nightmare. All we know for sure is what to avoid in order not to have bad dreams. We know, for instance, that we should not indulge in rich or heavy meals immediately before going to sleep. We also know that excessive drug use, including the mildest sleeping pill, as well as prolonged or excessive worry, can trigger the nightmare mechanism.

And psychologists also tell us to watch our thoughts immediately preceding the onset of sleep, for they are the most likely ones to surface during our dreams. Disagreeable or frightening subjects, morbid books and films, should all be carefully avoided shortly before going to sleep.

But what do you do if, after carefully avoiding all the suspected causes of the nightmares, you still find yourself battling Dracula and the Wolfman without the benefit of either a Crucifix or a silver bullet? The answer is simple. You must fight back. If Dracula bites you, bite him back. If the Wolfman is chasing you, turn around and give *him* a run for his money. Be as mean and nasty to your monsters as they are to you, meaner and nastier if possible. If you do, you will soon see that your nightmares are not darkening your sleeping times as often as they used to in the past.

> Woke at one, and lay melancholy till three or four – then sleeping, only to dream of finding a dead body of a child in a box, a little girl whom I had put living into it and forgotten.
>
> *– from John Ruskin's diary, 24 February 1885*

But wait, you say, how do I do these things, how do I control my nightmares? Easy. You tell yourself before going to sleep you do not wish to have any bad dreams, but that if they come, you will be prepared to fight them off.

What Do Nightmares Mean?

The reason why it is important for you to fight the nightmare is that *the frightening symbols that occur in a bad dream are in reality all the problems that you fear and the negative qualities within yourself you still have to overcome*. Whenever you face a threatening figure in a nightmare and vanquish it, you have successfully integrated a negative part of you or taken the first step to overcome a problem. You can be sure that specific figure will never threaten you or attack you again in a dream.

I would like to digress at this point and relate a nightmare I had recently which illustrates the preceding point. I dreamt with the archetype Jung called the Shadow, and which is the conglomeration of all the negative traits in the individual. When the Shadow is not fully integrated into the personality, it can destroy you. Unfortunately, its integration takes time and in some cases it is never accomplished.

In my dream, I saw the shadow of a woman moving stealthily about with a long knife, also in shadow, in her extended hand. I knew it was only a matter of time before it turned the knife on me. Almost immediately, I saw my hunch was right. The disembodied shadow turned around and lunged at me with raised knife. 'It's you I want to kill,' it hissed venomously at me. I was worried because I knew it could hurt me, but I held my ground. 'Why do you want to kill me?' I asked it. 'Because I hate you,' it answered, and moved closer. I still did not budge. And suddenly I was no longer frightened. I felt in total control of the situation in spite of the shadow's threat. 'No, you don't hate me,' I said. 'You love me. You love me very much, don't you?' The shadow lowered its head and the knife fell from its open hand. 'Yes, I do,' it said sadly. 'I love you very much. I just wish I were more like you, but I know that can never be.' It then drifted away and that was the end of the dream.

What happened during this dream was that I came face to face with all the negative aspects of my personality, accepted them, and most important of all, was able to control them, forcing them to realise they are still part of me and therefore should not hurt me. The shadow's sadness because it cannot be more like me is its acceptance that all of its traits must remain hidden because th :y are socially unacceptable. They can never be expressed consciously, hence, they 'can never be.' I was expressibly relieved with this dream because it marked a new growth in my personality and the integration of my shadow.

The Senoi and the Nightmare
The confrontation of threatening figures during nightmares is the life-long work of the Senoi tribe of the Malay Peninsula. This primitive people have been described by anthropologists as the most democratic group in man's history. They have had no violent crimes or personal conflicts for hundreds of years and are always happy and in perfect mental health.

The Senoi's secret for peace is simple. They use dream interpretation and manipulation for their mental health. The Senoi believe that dream images are part of the individual and are formed of pyschic forces that take external forms, like my dream of the shadow.

For this reason, they learn from childhood to master these internal forces. Senoi children are encouraged not only to confront, but actually to attack hostile figures or 'spirits' in their dreams. They are taught to call 'friendly spirits' to their aid during nightmares. These friendly forces, which can be equated with angelic and religious figures, are the positive inner aspects of the personality. The Senoi believe that any threatening figures destroyed by the dreamer will emerge later on as a friendly spirit or ally.

It is also important, according to the Senoi, not to be afraid of falling dreams. Confronted with such a dream, the individual should let himself fall, whereupon he will discover that the frightening falling dream turns into a pleasant flying experience, with its usually erotic under-tones.

Prolonged study of the dream beliefs of the Senoi has led many modern psychologists to conclude that their dream philosophy is the healthiest and most adequate for the preservation of mental health and the integration of the personality.

What has emerged from our brief study of the night-mare is that it is an expression of fears, anxieties and negative traits which we must try at all costs to control. This we can do simply by confronting the nightmare; instead of fearing it, we must attack it and ultimately vanquish it. By doing this we can succeed, not only in solving our problems but also in controlling all that is negative within us.

See back of book for dream forms and Dreamland blanket/duvet offer.

6. Can You Control Your Dreams?

*Those who dream by day are cognisant
of many things which escape those who dream by
night.*
– Edgar Allan Poe, Eleonora

We said in the previous chapter that ingesting a heavy meal before bedtime can be the cause of terrifying nightmares. Likewise, sounds that penetrate the subtle veil of sleep and are registered by the mind can influence our dreams in a variety of interesting ways. A dripping faucet can be incorporated into a dream as approaching or threatening footsteps, a doorbell can conjure images of weddings, messages or fires, running water can be transformed into waterfalls, floods or dreams of drowning.

In the same manner, the position of the body during sleep can influence a dream with startling results. A person may have dreams of being suffocated, dismembered or being engaged in any number of sexual activities simply by the pressure of bedclothes on his body.

Dreams of nakedness are also sparked by the weight of bedclothes or by being uncovered in a draughty bedroom.

All these dreams are known as a representative dreams, and are often caused by a specific type of automatic excitement of the brain region created by outside stimuli.

Very often, at the first onset of sleep, when a person if beginning to fall asleep, he or she may see a series of strange faces parading quickly before his/her eyes. Some-times other senses become involved as well, and the dreamer may seem to hear strange voices whispering in his/her ears or calling out his/her name. The feeling of being swallowed by rushing waters is not uncommon during these experiences.

Because of the eerie nature of these images and noises, many people ascribe mystical or supernatural meanings to these dreams. But again, they are the result of an overly active brain releasing a stream of unrelated images to the surface of the conscious mind. Faces and voices are most common because they are the simplest of all stored mental images and sounds.

Sleepwalking

The phenomenon of sleepwalking or somnambulism has baffled scientists for centuries. Together with bed-wetting and 'night terrors', sleepwalking occurs almost exclusively in small children and those in the pre-puberty stage. Although there have been some instances recorded of adults suffering from these disorders, these cases are quite rare.

Although most doctors agree that there is no definite clue as to the reason for sleepwalking, it has been suggested that these episodes may represent the expression of emotional conflicts that are repressed by the child during waking hours and allowed to be exteriorised during sleep. They can also be caused by hyperactivity in a child; in other words, a child that is always too active for his age and body build may often be the victim of sleepwalking.

Even today, dotor's advice on sleepwalking is not to treat it in any way, as the child will outgrow it before adolescence. Because most treatments are ineffective any-way, they serve only to make the child unnecessarily anxious.

'The human soul is a wonderful being and the central point of all its secrets is the dream.'

– Christian Friedrich Hebbel (1813–63)
German dramatist and lyric poet

What to do if you are an adult and you find yourself sleepwalking? Here the case is totally different. Sleepwalking in an adult is an indication of a severe anxiety that should be treated by a competent psychologist.

Induced Dreams

The induced dream is *a dream that is planted in the unconscious*. In other words, it is a way by means of which we can learn something about ourselves and our problems and how to solve them.

In the beginning, dreams were used as a means of preventing or curing diseases. Like Aristotle, who believed he could identify an illness by the type of dream dreamt by a person, most of the ancients believed that they could not only identify illnesses through dreams, but also cure them. Notable among the practitioners of dream medicine were Hippocrates and Galen, the fathers of modern medicine.

Inducing dreams in these early times was known as incubation. It consisted in going to a sacred place in order to receive a useful dream from a god. Although healing was one of the most important uses of the induced dream, the incubation was used for a variety of purposes.

For example, in the famous *Epic of Gilgamesh*, the hero appeals to a mountain for a dream shortly before attacking a monster. Gilgamesh and his companions use a magic ritual to achieve this purpose. They hollow out the ground facing the setting sun and from this hole emerges a mysterious sleep, maybe a drug-like vapour, which promptly overcomes the hero. The opening of the earth in this symbolic tale symbolises the unfolding of the unconscious processes to the conscious mind.

The Yogis also practice dream incubation in what they call the **intermediate** state of dreaming. Three conditions are necessary for the Yogi to evoke the dream desired.

First, during sleep the Yogi must never be unconscious, that is, he must be intensely aware that he is sleeping, and he must be able to control not only his dreams but the objects and people perceived in them.

Second, he must hold himself in a half sleep, the link between sleeping and waking.

And third, before going to sleep, he must do a series of breathing exercises that will place him at the required 'junction' between exhaled and inhaled breaths, at the very point were he enters into contact with pure energy. It is this energy that will produce the desired vision during sleep.

In Iran, the dervishes induce dreams by means of a drug mixed with wine. Muslims in general believe that the practice of incubation is part of a holy rite known as the **istiqara**. The dreams that result from this rite are believed to be divine revelations.

Two of the steps taken to induce this type of dream are, first of all, to invoke the aid and protection of the individual's eternal 'Master' and eternal 'Guide', and then to keep the mind from wandering while at the same time concentrating all thoughts on the desired dream.

Creative Dreaming

There are many cases in both literature and music where the ideas for either a literary or a musical masterpiece were found in a dream. For example, both *Treasure Island* and *Dr Jekyll and Mr Hyde* were inspired by dreams of Robert Louis Stevenson. Dante's *Divine Comedy*, Du Maurier's *Trilby* and Coleridge's *Kubla Khan* were all examples of masterpieces which were the result of dream inspiration.

Many other famous writers, such as Henry James, Baudelaire, Emily Brontë, Dostoyevsky, Wordsworth and Walter de la Mare, all used their dreams to write unforgettable literature.

Gottfreid Wilhelm Liebnetz (1646–1716), German rationalist, philosopher and mathematician, held that dreams are the products of accumulated memories since, he believed, nothing is ever forgotten.

Mental Suggestion through Dreams

Many modern psychologists are convinced that dreams cannot only be controlled by the dreamer, but also that his or her entire life may be altered by means of dreams. These psychologists believe that we can implant positive suggestions in our unconscious minds before going to sleep in order to get answers to our problems from the unconscious in the form of dreams.

Dr Patricia Garfield, a noted researcher in dream control, says that a dreamer who becomes totally aware of his/her dream state and can hold on to his/her awareness becomes capable of experiencing his/her heart's deepest desires in his/her dreams. He/she can 'consciously' choose to make love with the partner of his/her choice; he/she can travel in his/her dreams to distant lands; he/she can speak with any figure he/she wishes, real or fictional, dead or alive; he/she can find solutions to his/her waking problems; he/she can discover artistic creations.

The dreamer who can become 'conscious' in his/her dream state opens for him/herself an exciting personal adventure.

But perhaps most important of all, the creative dreamer's greatest advantage over the ordinary dreamer is his/her opportunity to unify and integrate his/her personality. The fearlessness of dream images that the creative dreamer learns to develop produces a mood of capability that carries over into waking life, providing a foundation for confident, capable action. Also, dream control will result in the ability to sustain dream images for long periods of time, as well as in an increasingly stronger capacity for dream recall.

How Do We Learn to Control Our Dreams?

Dr Garfield has not one, but half a dozen systems that a person can follow in order to make his/her dreams do as he/she wills. The simplest of these methods is the celebrated incubation system of the ancients. In the use of this method, the individual must begin by finding a particularly pleasant and harmonious place for his/her dream experiments, a place where he/she will not be distracted from the subject of his/her desired dream.

The next step to be followed is clearly to formulate the intended dream. It is important also to choose a specific dream topic, and to put one's intention into a concise, positive phrase, such as 'Tonight I learn how to solve this or that specific problem', taking care to specify clearly which problems one wishes to solve. One can also decide to have a dream about a special person or about how an illness may be cured.

The important thing to remember is that faith in the dream ritual and determination to succeed are the basic ingredients for the dream's success. One must be determined to receive an answer through a dream and keep

---

The wife of Joseph Conrad (1857–1924), the English novelist born in Poland, dreamed that her husband was thrown from a hansom cab when the horse slipped on a wet road. The next morning she received a message that Conrad had indeed been thrown from a cab and injured at exactly the same time his wife had had her dream.

concentration firmly anchored on the chosen dream topic.

The next thing to do after the preceding steps have been taken care of is deeply to relax the body through the rhythmic and periodic inhaling and exhaling of air. When the body is in a drowsy, relaxed state, one must repeat the chosen dream topic over and over, concentrating all thoughts on it. At this point, one visualises the dream as though it were about to happen, and tries to picture oneself after the dream has taken place. In other words, one must believe strongly that the unconscious mind can provide the desired dream.

Dr Garfield also counsels her students to record all their dreams in the present tense and to do so immediately upon awakening. She also believes it is important to produce positive dream images in some form in waking life. Specifically, she advises to engage in activities related to the desired dream just before going to sleep. This will ensure that the unconscious will receive a clear visual image connected with the dream before sleep, making it easier to achieve the desired dream goal.

Some people have the uncanny ability to wake up in the middle of the night, interrupting a pleasurable dream, and then go back into the dream and continue it where they left off. This type of dream control can also be acquired with perseverance and determination. But perhaps the most desirable aspect of dream control would be to become aware that we are dreaming in the middle of a dream. This is known as the lucid dream and is a common practice among Yogis.

There are several known steps to achieve the lucid dream. First of all, you must accept that all dreams are thought forms. This means that every horrible nightmare and shocking dream you ever had was only an expression of your own unconscious mind. Knowing this will make it easier for you to confront a monster in a nightmare and will not leave you so dismayed if you find yourself in an amorous dalliance with a particularly disturbing partner.

The next step in achieving the lucid dream is to determine to remain conscious during your dreams. It is very helpful if you concentrate on the idea of dream consciousness for two or three days before attempting to become aware during a dream. As you become conscious during a dream, you can induce any change you want in it. This will render your fearless of any dream image, no matter how terrifying, because you will have the ability to change that image at will. As you become unafraid of negative symbolism in dreams, you will be able to use your dreams for creative and healing purposes.

Above all, you must remember that, as in all things, achieving control in dreams requires persistence and the determination to succeed. As in the old adage, remember, if at first you don't succeed, try, try again. Eventually you will.

The natives of New Guinea distinguish between 'free' dreams and official dreams. The latter are taken seriously as giving advice before the dreamer carries out some enterprise in real life. 'Free' dreams are those to which no particular significance is attached.

---

7. How to Interpret Your Dreams

There's a long, long night of waiting
Until all my dreams come true,
Till the day when I'll be going
Down that long, long trail with you.
– Stoddard King, 'There's a Long, Long Trail'

As we have seen, some of our dreams do come true. And this happens because the human unconscious moves on a space-time continuum where past, present and future blend into infinity. The prophetic of prospective dream is part of the phenomenon Jung called synchronicity, which we discussed in Chapter 5. There is no doubt that the prophetic dream does take place. What is curious is the fact that not all of our dreams come true and that we are seldom able to foretell ahead of time which of our dreams are prophetic and which are not.

The Prophetic Dream
What all prophetic dreams have in common is a quality of forewarning. Nothing of real importance happens to us that is not foretold somehow in a dream. And invariably, this dream also prepares us or in some way suggests what we must do about a forthcoming event.

When the event foretold by a dream is either disagreeable or tragic, it is as if the unconscious were telling us by means of the dream that we should be strong and prepare ourselves for a disastrous occurrence. What seems to take place then is a strengthening of the mental and emotional aspect of an individual. Because he or she has already lived the negative experience in a dream, he/she is better prepared to face it in reality. In this sense we could say that the prophetic dream cushions an individual against sudden shocks that could be threatening to his/her physical and mental well-being. Likewise, exciting or joyous events are often foretold in dreams because they can also be taxing emotionally and physically to an individual.

How to Handle Bad Dreams

First of all, we must try to determine if the bad dream was the result of a heavy meal ingested just before going to sleep. If this was not the case, we can then proceed to identify the dream motifs and try to interpret their symbolism. If we discern a message in the dream symbols we can then try to adopt whichever protective measures we can, if there are any. If there are none, we should then try to relax and take the dream at face value.

It is simply useless to worry about a bad dream because we can never tell which ones are prophetic and which ones are simply an expression of negative trends in our mental makeup. And in any case, the prophetic dream can seldom be averted. It simply foretells something that is going to happen and over which we have no control.

Dream Analysis

We said earlier that our dreams are symbolic images released by the unconscious mind during sleep. We also said that we can control these images in a variety of ways, such as mental suggestion. However, these images cannot be implanted in the unconscious unless they belong to the individual's actual experience. For example, you cannot expect to dream of the Champs Elysées in all its glory if you have never been to Paris. In other words, the unconscious can only work with material that has been stored within it through previous experience.

According to *Mother Bridget's Wisdom*, an eighteenth-century tract, to know your future:

On the first of January: before going to bed drink a pint of cold spring water into which you have beaten the yolk of a pullet's egg, the legs of a spider and the pounded skin of an eel, and your destiny will be revealed in a dream.

On St Agnes Night (21 January): take a row of pins, and pull out every one, one after another, saying a Paternoster, sticking a pin in your sleeve, and you will dream of the one you shall marry.

On Lady Day (25 March): string thirty-one nuts on a string composed of red worsted mixed with blue silk and tie it around your neck on going to bed, repeating these lines:

> Oh, I wish! Oh, I wish to see
> Who my true love is to be!

Shortly after midnight you will see your lover in a dream, and at the same time be informed of all of the principal events of your future.

On St Swithin's Eve (14 July): write down the three things you most wish to know, using a new pen filled with red ink, on a sheet of fine-woven paper from which you have previously cut off – and burnt – the corners. Fold the paper in a true lover's knot and wrap it around three hairs from your head. Place the paper under your pillow for three successive nights, and your dreams will tell your future.

Dream Motifs

We mentioned earlier the symbols that recur in everyone's dreams and which Jung called dream motifs. Examples of the dream motifs are dreams about trains, weddings, flying, climbing, falling and hundreds of other subjects. These are the dreams that compose the typical dream dictionaries, such as the one included in this book.

When we analyse a dream we must try to identify as many motifs as there are in the dream. So if we dream we are running down a flight of stairs in the pursuit of a soldier who has just shot a stranger, we should be able to identify four motifs: 1. Stairs; 2. Shooting; 3. Soldier; and 4. Stranger.

We then find the traditional meanings associated with each of these motifs as given in a dream dictionary.

Next, we concentrate on each motif and write down the first thing that comes to our minds in connection with that particular subject. This will reveal to us what individual meaning each motif has for us. This meaning may vary from one person to another.

You should make a habit of recording the actual experiences you associate with certain dream motifs or symbols. For example, if you discover that shortly after dreaming of a rose you get a letter with pleasant news, you should record this experience, and take it into consideration whenever you see roses in your dreams. If you are careful in the compilation of your dream record, it should not be very long before you have put together your very own dream dictionary that applies only to you.

The Sleep Ritual

Most of us go to sleep every night too tired or sleepy to follow any given ritual. We take sleeping habits for granted, as well as our dreams. But, in reality, our sleeping periods are every bit as important as our waking periods because during sleep we adjust to and assimilate the conflicts we face during our waking time. This is done, as we have seen, through the symbology of dreams. It is, therefore, very important to go to sleep every night in the proper frame of mind. A short sleep ritual is the best way to accomplish this, and all of us, no matter how tired or how busy, can find the time to conduct such a ritual. It does not take very long, and the difference can change our lives.

The sleep ritual suggested here is quite simple. The first thing to do once you are in bed and ready to go to sleep is to lie flat on your back with eyes closed and arms resting alongside your body, starting with your feet and moving upward slowly until you have relaxed the muscles of your head and scalp. While you are relaxing each group of muscles you should be breathing deeply and evenly.

When your body feels comfortable and relaxed, you should proceed to implant in your unconscious whatever suggestion you desire to take place during your dreams. At this point, you should tell yourself that you wish to remember all important dreams upon awakening and that you will not be afraid of any dream you may have, no matter how disagreeable. This is all you need to do. It is simple, easy and short, but you will feel the difference in the positive quality of your next dreams. Because some people may fall asleep during the relaxation and deep breathing period, some psychologists recommend implanting your suggestions first and then proceeding with the muscle relaxation.

If you wish to contact someone on the unconscious level during sleep, you can do it also at the time of our sleep ritual by simply stating your intention to meet this person during your sleep and seeing the outcome of the meeting in a dream.

Remember at all times that dreams are not only messages but also accurate records of the state of your unconscious mind. Their main purpose is to make your life easier and more bearable, and to give you more control over your destiny. By understanding your dreams, you will not only understand yourself better but will also understand others and their relationships to you.

Through proper dream analysis your horizons will expand and your chances of success will increase a hundredfold. We have shown you how to achieve these goals. Put the acquired knowledge to good use, and may you have many happy dreams.

Part II

A–Z Dream Dictionary

Charles Alverson

The Author

Charles Alverson is an American author and journalist who has lived in Britain for twenty years. In addition to publishing three novels for adults, two for young adults and two for children, he was co-author of the film, *Jabberwocky*. As a journalist, he has written for the *Sunday Times*, *Sunday Telegraph*, *Wall Street Journal*, *International Herald Tribune* and a wide range of general interest magazines. Though not trained in psychology, he has long been fascinated by dreams from a personal and analytical point of view and his readings on the subject have been wider and more ecclectic than they have been disciplined.

Introduction

Who has not woken from a vivid dream with the thought: 'What a curious dream. I wonder what it means'? There is a strong desire to understand our dreams, which is reflected by the saying of an early Talmudic rabbi: 'A dream that is not understood is like a letter that is not opened.' And we all know how maddening an unopened letter can be.

If only understanding our dreams were as simple as opening and reading letters. For a start, as much as we claim to want to unlock the mystery of our dreams, very few of us ever systematically record our dreams or make a serious attempt to unravel the clues therein. Those who do will discover that the land of dreams and their interpretation is a complex and shifting terrain. It is not that interpreting dreams is difficult. It is all too easy. A search through the popular press will turn up a great many examples of the *If you dream of eating apples, you have bad (or good) luck* school of dream interpretation. I think you will agree that this is too simple by far.

The one thing on which most people who have seriously studied dreams and their meanings agree is that *every* dream means something. The problem is that very

> A short time before he was assassinated, American President Abraham Lincoln dreamed that he was awoken from his sleep by mournful sounds and sobbing. In his dream, Lincoln went downstairs in the White House and heard more sobbing but saw no-one until he entered a state room and found a catafalque with a corpse upon it wrapped in funeral vestments and with its face covered.
>
> 'Who is dead in the White House?' he demanded.
>
> 'The president,' was the answer. 'He was killed by an assassin.'
>
> Lincoln then awoke, and within two weeks he was dead from the bullet of John Wilkes Booth and lying in state in that same room.

few interpreters agree on exactly what that meaning is. Even Professor C. G. Jung, the noted Swiss psychologist who considered dreams one of the most important clues to the wonders of the human mind, found it difficult to be very exact on the subject. Consider his pronouncement: 'If we meditate on a dream sufficiently long and thoroughly, if we carry it around with us and turn it over and over, something almost always comes of it.'

I think that most readers will agree that this statement from one of the best known and regarded practitioners of the arcane practice of dream unravelling is far from the simplistic sort of interpretation one is sometimes offered. In my own case, an intense desire to understand something of the content and origins of my dream led me to may sources. Far from leading to easy solutions, I have to admit that my reading on dreams and their meanings has raised for me considerably more questions than answers. Nor would I claim for my guides to the interpretation of various dream elements in this book any unique wisdom. No less an authority than Havelock Ellis, the author of many works on psychology and dreams, believed that 'We can never go behind the fantastic universe of our dreams. The validity of that universe is, for dreaming consciousness, unassailable.'

A Dream Come True

In general most of my dreams night and day are focused on the impossibility of making out as a footballer. However, you will be pleased to hear that at last part of this dream will be coming true on May 21st at Wimbledon FC where the Charity side I run, Walford Boys Club, will be playing Wimbledon to raise money for Barnardo's.

— Tom Watt

Anyone who has dipped into the writing of Sigmund Freud on the subject of dreams will find that many of *his* interpretations are couched in sexual terms as expressions of primary instincts, the symbols of unrecognised fears and wishes. This has led to a 'school' of dream interpretation which simplistically relates almost every element of a dream to some aspect of the dreamer's sexuality. This. I believe, is taking Freud's powerful insight into the human psyche too far and dangerously narrowing what started out as a broad understanding of human nature.

On the other hand, there is the theory of dream interpretation which insists that dreams serve as a portent of something which, if the dreamer only understood it, could unlock the key to the future. This was highly useful in times when religion and psychology were used as political tools, and a ruler could conveniently have his wizard or magician interpret dreams to serve the ruler's ends. The Iroquois Indians of North America and the ancient Greeks both found predictive value in dreams. The judges of the Holy Inquisition used alleged interpretations of dreams to sentence alleged witches to be burnt at the stake. It is perhaps a tribute to modern society that such extreme uses and valuations of dreams are no longer common. People who let their dreams of the night before guide their decisions and actions at work or school would be taking some interesting risks.

This is not to say that dreams cannot contain important messages. Samuel Taylor Coleridge claimed to have dreamt the entirety of his classic poem, *Kubla Khan*, possibly under the influence of opium. Robert Louis Stevenson supposedly received the plots of his novels through his dreams. Frederich Kekule, the mid-Victorian chemist, conceived of the structure of the benzene ring through a dream he had of a snake with its tail in its mouth forming a circle. This is all the more reason for those who suspect themselves of harbouring genius to record their dreams carefully. But it is far easier to remember some

---

The Computer Game

I was in bed. It was 1 o'clock. After a long time I fell asleep. I had an awful nightmare. I was playing on my computer. I had loaded a game called 'robot war', then suddenly I felt myself shrinking, I fell on the keyboard. The next time I could see I was three centimetres high. I was on the computer deck. The joystick was next to me. I looked the other way and saw the computer screen; on it was a lifeless planet with robots running around on it, and a man with a space suit on and a laser gun blowing the robots to pieces. Suddenly I fell into a hole in the side of the computer. The next moment I was on a desolate wasteland with robots running around. Then I saw a robot coming towards me with hands out. I could do nothing but run. I ran. It was closing in on me fast. Then I felt my neck being squeezed. I screamed. Then I was in bed again, awake, sweating, tired.

Nicholas Monk
Shiplake C.E. School
Age 11

Heaven or Hell

I am playing in a football match and am by far the best player on the field, winning the game virtually on my own, and being praised by all around me.

(DH used to play in a showbiz football team.)

I have died and gone to hell and hell is a loud disco with flashing lights, a never ending thumping beat, a smell of stale beer and a thick fog of cigarette smoke. This is a recurring 'nightmare' from which I nearly always wake up in a cold sweat.

(DH has spent a large part of his working life in discos.)

– David Hamilton

aspects of your dream than to interpret them with any degree of exactitude.

Perhaps the most difficult part of dream interpretation is that dreams are very rarely simple. A careful recording of the details of a dream could easily turn up several major elements which could be crucial to its interpretation. Which are important, and which can be put aside? Perhaps two elements in your dream cancel each other out, allowing a third to assume predominant importance. You might even overlook the most important, if subtle, element of your dream while chasing up dead-end avenues littered with apparently obvious symbols.

Amongst the first things I discovered when I began trying to interpret my dreams was that – with minor exceptions – dreams are made of the flimsiest substance imaginable. So often, retaining them is like trying to grab a handful of fog. Countless times, I have awoken with a dream of utmost clarity and vividness imprinted on my brain. But by the time I'd brushed my teeth all I had left was a very strong *feeling* that I'd had a remarkable dream and only the scantiest memory of its details.

Thus, I learned the hard way to record my dreams

instantly on waking. A notebook and pencil on the bedside cabinet – with a light, of course, for use when a vivid dream literally wakes you in the middle of the night – will suffice, but I found that the more system I applied to setting down the details of my dreams, the more luck I had trying to unravel them. Mind you, you could probably spend all day recording very single detail of a fresh and colourful dream. I compromised by developing a short, but detailed, form for each dream I recorded (*see next page with spares at the back of this book*).

In this simple form, I try to capture as much pertinent detail from the dream as can be remembered, along with whatever emotional content the dream had for me. There is, of course, no guarantee that you will be able to do anything very practical with this material, but one thing is for sure, if you don't recall the details of your dreams, your chances of understanding them are very slight indeed.

As you will see from the alphabetical listings of suggested interpretations I give in this book, I lean heavily on intuition and symbolic representations. Since, as I see it, dreams are the by-product of physical, emotional and psychological experience, they must be interpreted in light of both our real and symbolic understanding of the world. For instance, if a dream strongly features ASHES (see listing

The Praise of Men

I have always dreamt of being selected for Wales at Rugby.

I have often dreamt of walking out at Cardiff Arms Park to the roar of fifty thousand Welshmen.

I probably think of this as the thing I would like to do most in my life, so it often creeps into my dreams.

– Terry Griffiths

on page 89) I believe one must think of them not only literally – as the remains of something now destroyed by fire – but metaphorically as symbols of loss, perhaps guilt. Only the individual can truly interpret the significance of a particular element of his or her dream. Gurus and guides can help, but only as far as the dreamer can accept such help. They are *your* dreams.

To me the most important elements of a dream lie not in the detail but in the context of that detail and how you – the dreamer – *felt* about it. Dreams are perhaps the most individual aspect of the human personality, the fingerprints of the soul, a unique spiritual DNA pattern. Even two identical dreams – if such exist – could mean totally different things to different dreamers. In trying to understand and interpret your dreams, you are working with absolutely unique material. For anyone – especially an artist or a scientist – a very exciting idea.

Finally, I hope you enjoy this book and your effort to understand your dreams – and perhaps yourselves – better. But dream interpretation is not a science. It's just one of a myriad of man's efforts to bring some order into the infinite elements of the human mind and soul. Don't look for miracles and you may discover a small one.

Charles Alverson
Cambridge, England
July 1989

Caught Short

My recurring dream is that I'm out in the street, being chased by hundreds of people. I'm wearing a very short vest...and I can't pull the front down!

– *Ernie Wise*

DREAM RECORDING FORM

Date: _____ **Time (if known):** _____
What happened: _____
_____
_____
_____
_____
_____
_____

Dream Details:
Day or night? _____ Season, if any? _____
Predominant colours recalled: _____
_____
Primary emotions recalled: _____
_____
Physical sensations (if any): _____
_____
Familiar persons, animals, objects: _____
_____
Miscellaneous: _____
_____
Mood on awakening: _____
_____
_____
_____

(with the other side of the page blank for other observations)

Peanut Crunch

If I wake up and discover that I haven't been dreaming, I feel cheated somehow. Like I've missed the big movie.

I tend to have abstract dreams and encounter situations that I never would in real life. Like when I was a small boy, the first dream I ever remember having was standing alone in the schoolyard on a brilliantly sunny day hanging around on the school steps. Suddenly I heard a low rumbling sound and to my amazement saw, coming around the corner, a gigantic peanut rolling towards me. It must have been fifty feet high. One of those wrinkly things with a peanut at each end. I remember it rolled right over me. To this day, I can't imagine why I had this dream.

Nowadays, I always dream in colour of course as I can see no point in not doing so. A black-and-white dream would be too arty and peculiar.

Sometimes I dream about royalty. Mostly the Queen. Well, why not go straight to the top? I once dreamed She was lying in the street with her handbag over her arm. I rushed over to help her up but she quickly declined saying, 'No, no. I have people to do this for me!' In some dream situations I chicken out from doing really adventurous things like skiing down a steep mountain and when I wake up, I feel like a creep for not having gone ahead and done it. Or maybe I dream I'm at a horrible party and instead of just walking out and doing something more interesting, I'll stay, just out of courtesy. When I wake up from a dream like that, I'm annoyed at myself for putting up with bad situations or not being adventurous. I think there's a lesson there that I should transfer to my waking life.

Anyway, I love dreams. They don't hurt like real life sometimes does, they're interesting to relate in conversation, and how else do you get to meet the Queen!

— *Kenny Everett*

A–Z Dream Dictionary

A

Abandoned Dreaming that you have been abandoned or left behind may be a sign that you are newly independent or on the verge of independence and thus feel insecure.

Abyss To find yourself near an abyss in your dream can be an omen of impending danger, a symbol of warning. If you actually fall into the abyss, it can be a metaphor for inner aloneness and wretchedness, an intimation of emptiness in your life and lack of hope. Being *pushed* – by a known or unknown force – into the abyss can reflect your need to explore the depths of your unconscious.

Accident If it happens to you, this may symbolise guilt or self-punishment; if someone else is the victim – especially someone you recognise – it would mean you feel hostility towards that person.

Accidents in social situation These may suggest that you feel insecure or nervous in a situation in which you might seem in total control.

Animals (various species)
Very young animals: this may represent you in an effort to reject responsibility.
Bear: this could symbolise someone who has tried to dominate you in your life.
Cat: this image could reflect the sinuous, catlike, slightly exotic side of your personality.
Cow: the fact that this animal is clearly associated with milk and nurturing makes it a common symbol of the maternal figure in your life.
Dinosaur: this another animal evoking images of the ancient past could refer to something from your very early childhood.
Dog: this animal may suggest some individual who you would like to get away from but who seems to insist on following you; if it is a dog you recognise, this could mean that the dog stands in for its owner; to dream of a dog from your past suggests nostalgia for an earlier time in your life.
Domesticated Animal: this may be an indication that your passions are under a deep – seated and habitual control which seems impossible to shake off.
Elephant: a symbol of stolidity and substance which could

A Newscaster's Nightmare

My recurrent dream is of a TV studio outside which I'm standing, unable to get in. It is full of water. I can't get through the door. It is one minute to ten. The news begins. I am not there.

– Carol Barnes

represent something or someone to whom you look for connection with reality.

Frog: this animal, noted for the transformation it undergoes, could symbolise a major or intergral change in your life.

Hare: see Rabbit.

Horse: this dream image is strongly suggestive of harnessed power under your control; a dream about a horse which is straining without result or apparently weakening could relate to your fear of losing power.

Horse (dead): in contradiction, this image could suggest a lucky event coming to your life.

Lion: this can symbolise raging physical appetites, unfightable force or desire; if your dream portrays you struggling with a lion and winning, this could indicate a success in your process of maturing.

Lizard: can be taken as a sign of obsession with one particular course of action or thinking.

Monkey: the appearance of this primate in your dreams often indicates that you fear that your behaviour is childish or tending to regress to a more primitive level.

Monster or other mythical creature: such a beast can symbolise a distant but real fear which you cannot really understand; if you seem to be immune to the monster or capable of vanquishing it, this could indicate overcoming fear of the unknown of death.

Oxen (fat): a common symbol of wealth and prosperity.

Oxen (ploughing): these work animals can be taken as a symbol

The Poem of Dreams

Dreaming dreams is really quite fun,
If you dream you're a mum.
Dreaming can be terrible. If you dream your school has added on some more extra terms,
And then if you are made to bathe in a bath full of worms.
Sometimes in your dreams you are made to say sorry.
Sometimes in your dreams you are made to work in a quarry.
You may find in your dreams you're floating down a big wide stream.
But don't forget that dreams are not real. Even if you dream
You had a meal and woke up in the night,
Tasting in your mouth tender meat, roast potatoes and a drink of sprite.

Lucy Potter
Shiplake Primary School
Age 9

Dr Thomas Barnardo's Dream

It seemed to me that I was walking by the side of a dark and rapid stream, when suddenly I heard a cry for help. Turning quickly round, I saw a boy in the middle of the water, which was carrying him swiftly down. He was drowning, and he could not help himself. As quickly as I could I ran along the bank so as to get in front of him, calling the while for aid to save him. When I got below him, I threw myself down upon the brink of the river and stretched out my arms to reach him. Alas! My arms were not nearly long enough! I thought I could not swim and I was afraid to venture into the water myself, lest both of us should be drowned. I had no rope, and there was nobody passing. All at once I caught sight of some children away down the bank playing under one of the trees. I called as loudly as I could, but I had hardly time to notice if they heard me. I stretched myself out once more, to be ready to reach the poor boy who was drifting nearer and nearer, but I saw that he was still beyond my reach and if I stretched out any farther I should certainly overbalance myself and be lost.

Just then I heard a child's voice behind me "We will hold you, sir; don't be afraid!" I felt children's hands catch my feet, and then grasp my garments, so as to let me reach out nearer to the drowning lad. Yes, thank God, I could touch him. I had him in my grip, and in another moment, though it seemed an age, my child-helpers were pulling me and my burden as hard as they could, until they drew us in from the water on to the bank. The boy was safe! And I felt such a thrill of satisfaction at the thought that I awoke.

Ah, but I knew what my dream meant! For it was a parable as well as a dream. I could not save the poor helpless little waif of the street by myself: I had not enough money: I had not enough strength: my arms were not long enough. But the children, happy and safe, were going to hold me and lend me their strength, courage, and readiness for the great rescue work. I resolved forthwith that I would try to bind boys and girls into a LEAGUE, which would save, not one poor child from drowning in the river, but thousands of homeless and forlorn children who were living lives of darkness and sorrow!

of effort which leads to gain or treasure.

Pig or Wild Boar: this image may indicate that you recognise the selfish, over-consuming and heedless side of your nature. A pig seen in an incongruously rich surrounding may suggest a realisation of false or material values.

Rabbits: widely considered a strong symbol of fertility, but if you note that the animal is a hare, this can suggest an increase in spiritual awareness or understanding.

Rat: a primal fear symbol of all that is repulsive, perhaps an image standing for a particular person who you think 'ratted' on you.

Actor No matter how unlike yourself, the actor you dream about could well be you. Your subconscious may be trying to tell you that in some aspect of your life you are behaving in a forced or unnatural manner.

Aggression If you feel that the aggression in your dream is directed towards yourself, you may feel threatened in some aspect of your waking life, possibly from an unexpected person or source; if this aggression is manifested towards you while you are seemingly safe, you may be longing to escape what seems to be smothering overprotection.

Angel A symbol of unattainable purity and flawlessness which may sometimes be paired with the familiar image of the devil or some other symbol of evil. When so paired, this may suggest the contrasting elements in your own nature or which face you in a given situation. Sometimes the angel may distress you by behaving most unangelically, which represents the same contradiction.

Animals Animals in your dreams may reflect a wide range of influences from your waking life. A dream of escaping from an animal – especially a wild one – could symbolise an inner struggle with your own animal instincts; if you're taming the animal, it could correlate to your attempts to quell your own animal instincts and direct them; if you're killing the animal, it could be signs of your too rigid efforts at controlling your basic instincts; eating the animal you have killed may be a wish that you could take on its inherent energy; if you find yourself talking with the animal or animals in your dream, it could reflect your wish to delve into a pure source of knowledge; if, in turn, the animal seems to be trying to help *you*, it could mean that something in your unconscious mind is trying to be revealed to you through this means; if the animal does not seem to realise that you are even

Dream of a crocodile, wake to danger
Dream of a lobster and wake to wealth
Dream of a dog and you'll meet a stranger
Dream of a frog and you'll know good health

Dream of a squirrel – your hopes mount higher
Dream of an eagle and grow to fame
Dream of a wolf and you'll meet a liar
(Dream mice or monkeys for much the same)

Dream of a bear and it's odd agin' you
Dream of a bull and a rival's there
Dream of a swan and pleasure will win you
Dream of a shark and you'll know despair

Dream of beetles and worries arise
Dream of a fish for a nice surprise

– English folk poem

A Recurring Dream

A long time ago my peaceful slumbers were disturbed by a recurring nightmare that visited me about once a year. My teeth began to crumble and drop out, one by one. Then I would wake up, all in a blether, feel them carefully and find, to my great relief, that they were all still firmly in place. As the years went by, this nightmare became ever more perverse, for I would dream that I had woken up to find – oh horror! – that they really *had* fallen out! In time it reached the stage when I was convinced that the dream of a dream was itself a dream, and that I was indeed quite toothless.

Happily, these horrible fantasies have ceased…and I *still* have a full set of gnashers!

– Victoria Gillick

there, this could indicate some inner self - absorption you are fighting against.

Serpent: *See* Monster. defeating or slaying a monster can symbolise victory over heavy odds.

Sheep: considered an image of the passive and conforming side of the dreamer's nature, but may also be a symbol of self-disgust or stifled rebellion.

Snake: a sexual threat of perhaps a person the dreamer fears in a sexual way; if the dreamer seems to be attracted to the snake, it could be a sign of sexual ambivalence.

Toad: often an image which suggests the dreamer's vision of the unattractive side of his nature or personality.

Unicorn: a very strong sign that the dreamer sees the prospect of resolving inner anguish or recognises beauty in an unexpected way.

Vermin in a place you consider your own: this symbol could mean you fear unwelcome guests, resent younger symbols or even an unwanted pregnancy.

Wild Animals: a clear symbol of natural passions as well as of danger to the dreamer from an outside source. If the seemingly wild animal is then seen to be tame, this could indicate that such passions and fears are being overcome.

Wolf: very often stands for cruel fantasies which the dreamer feels are beyond conscious control.

Wounded Animal: a likely personification of the dreamer's dread of abasement or physical harm.

Ascending If you seem – perhaps magically – to be moving physically to a higher realm, this could symbolise recognition of internal development to a more refined state.

Ashes (*charred remains*) Can be a sign of contrition or acceptance of guilt, or of recognition of humiliation. Ashes can also symbolise peace or resignation after a turbulent time.

Attitudes It is best to be cautious of too literally accepting your seeming mood or attitude in a dream. Dreams are seldom that simple and an apparent emotion can be a mask to hide the dreamer's real attitude towards some event or anticipated happening. Consider the opposite attitude for its relevance.

Axe (or crude sword) May be a symbol of separation or a parting from old habits or surroundings. Try to be aware of your apparent feelings about this image.

A Midnight Gallop

I am galloping over the turf through a field. Earth flies up on either side of me. I can hear the sound of the magnificent stallion's heart against my chest – trees shoot past on either side. It starts to pour with rain. The clouds become black and thunder rolls. We gallop on through the fields. We charge down hill, past a wood. A tree falls in our path, struck by lightning. The white stallion rears and clears the fallen tree with a mighty leap and we gallop on into the increasing darkness. The shape of a river lies in front of us. I urge the tremendous animal on and we charge through the lake. Water flies up on either side of me. At last we reach the other side. The thud of the hooves continues rapidly. It is like a nightmare, yet it was more magnificent than scary yet it feels terrifying. We charge on through the fields. The night begins to fade. An old, gnarled oak shoots past. We are galloping up a hill, we reach the top and charge down the hill. The horse's hooves beat the ground underfoot. We are galloping faster and faster. Suddenly the shape of a black horse appears. My steed rears in fury, bellows and charges towards the black stallion. I have never experienced such magnificence as on that night. Many people would say it was a dream or a nightmare, but whatever you decide to call it, I'll never forget the thud of the great beast's hooves against the ground and the rhythm of the white stallions heart on that midnight gallop.

John Steward
Shiplake Primary School
age 9

B

Baby This is an image which can reflect an aspect of your own nature, the child within us all which needs to be protected. In certain circumstances, the appearance of a baby in your dream can represent your yearning to start again, to give up old ways.

Ball Its circular nature makes the ball a symbol of completeness, of your life as a whole. But other interpretations of this image involve potency, pregnancy and fecundity.

Bank This is a symbol of security and could suggest your longing for emotional strength and safety.

Barn (*overflowing with grain*) This symbol can signify marriage to a wealthy mate and general abundance.

Bathing In clean water an auger of good fortune; in dirty or muddy water an omen of bad luck and ill tidings.

Bees If, in your dream, you find yourself following a swarm of bees, this could betoken imminent gain or profit.

Beheading This morbid image could indicate fear of losing mental ability or could be symbolic of the painful abandonment of emotion for more intellectual pursuits.

Bells This dream image or sound could tell you that your conscience is nagging you, reminding you of duty.

Birds A flock of birds could be a dream image for lofty thoughts or imagination. Specific types of birds or birds in given situations or settings can have a variety of interpretations: a bird, perhaps a jackdaw, entering a house could signify loss.

A bird with clipped wings: could symbolise thwarted aspirations or dreams.

Chicken: could represent a flight of imagination kept firmly to earth by necessity.

Crow: can be taken as a symbol for the black-robed priest or, if especially sombre, death.

Eagle: a symbol of the free, unfettered spirit and can indicate a will to command others.

Eagles flying overhead: could be taken as a symbol of evil fortune or a shadow on your future.

Owl: this mysterious nightbird can represent the soul of the dead, but is also a well-known symbol of wisdom.

Peacock: a showy symbol of regeneration and wholeness of being, but, more specifically, could stand for a particularly handsome individual.

Phoenix: a mythical and widespread symbol for a recovery from destruction and devastation.

Raven: widely considered to represent evil, perhaps the devil or other dark and shadowy creature.

Wild Goose: this high flier can symbolise the liberation of the spirit, perhaps when the dreamer is feeling trapped or inhibited.

Birth If a married woman who is not pregnant dreams of having a baby, this can have portent of future motherhood; if a single woman has this dream, it can mean she has important rituals and celebrations coming. But not all birth dreams need be so literal. If the dreamer is crawling in or out of tunnels, holes, narrow channels, this can be a symbolic birth in expectation of some important transition or event.

Body (parts of the)

Abdomen or rib cage: can represent the inhibition of feeling and emotions, especially dark forbodings.

Blood: This liquid can symbolise the wellspring of life, the spirit as well as more ethereal aspects; a bath of blood, though a gory image, can be indicative of transition (baptism) into an adult state. Bloody teeth in ancient times were taken to signify the death of the dreamer.

Eye: a symbol for the window of the soul or insight into true feelings or thoughts. Blindness, permanent or temporary, may be a sleeping reminder of loss of understanding or intuition, and regaining vision a symbol of renewed insight.

Hair: a common symbol for feelings or virility or strength, but unexpected baldness or the – perhaps forced – cutting of the dreamer's hair can indicate fear of incipient weakness.

Hands: these largely symbolise creativity and craftsmanship, the ability to create manually; if the two hands are in sharp contrast, either in size or in what they hold, this could stand for uncertain examination of alternatives.

Head: a mature head on a child's body can symbolise someone who is more grown up mentally than physically or sexually. In addition, the representation of the head or skull may symbolise the dreamer's deliberate intentions, and an injury to the head could mean the dreamer feels blocked or defeated by outside forces.

Mouth: often symbolises the physical absorption of mental concepts such as understanding.

Nose: an emphasis on this organ can indicate that the dreamer senses that something is wrong or false and seeks to gain a true understanding.

Skin: a useful image for the dreamer's outward self-presentation to others. If the skin seems hard and unyielding, this may indicate a desire to have a defence against the world.

Teeth: these are both symbols of weapons and, in the case of teeth which are loose or falling out, can also represent either maturation or fear of aging.

Tongue: if seemingly out of control, this image can connote a fear of revealing a secret.

Books (whether in a library or a bookshop) Since books contain ideas, they can be an allegory for the thoughts and memories of the dreamer.

Box A strong symbol of confinement, the box can represent fear of anything from imprisonment to portents of death, suggesting a coffin.

Breaking Either the sound or the image of something breaking can be an image evocative of the destruction of certain ideals or standards.

Bridge Can signify successful undertakings or transitions, quite possibly a major change; but a broken bridge indicates fear and trouble and warns the dreamer to beware the unknown road.

Bulldozers This modern image could be the literal representation of the dreamer's fear of the external danger to ideals or inhibitions.

Buried alive Far from representing death, this image harks back to the experience of birth as recorded on the unconscious.

Sweet Dreams

I had a dream that I was in a world of sweets and we used to eat a bit of a house. My favourite was the House of Parliament. It had a stick of rock bended into an arch shape for the sides of the door and the door was chocolate as was the chimney. The windows were made of icing, the roof was chocolate and the smoke was candyfloss. You go through the chocolate door and there are two chairs. The cushions are strawberry jam and the gold lining is fudge. The floor is solid rock. I used to slide along the floor with my tongue out to lick the floor.

– Oliver Gaudion
Shiplake Primary School

C

Candle A candle being lighted forecasts an impending birth; to exhibit a vigorously burning candle presages contentment and prosperity; a flickering candle can indicate sickness, sadness and decay.

Cannibalism A dream about this social taboo can symbolise a desire to acquire the wealth, intellect or virtues of some other person. This image can also connote a devouring passion for another person.

Being carried May indicate the dreamer's urge to go back to the state of babyhood and helplessness, a desire to make the bare minimum of personal effort.

Castle This symbol of strength and resistance may represent a woman at her most formidable.

Caves These can be symbolic of the inner resources of the mind, the source of mystery and healing. Going down into a cave can indicate a pragmatic descent from a too-elevated conscious position; dread of not finding the way out of a cave could indicate fear of insanity.

'I'm afraid he'll catch cold with lying on the damp grass,' said Alice, who was a very thoughtful little girl.

'He's dreaming now,' said Tweedledee: 'And what do you think he's dreaming about?'

Alice said: 'Nobody can guess that.'

'Why, about *you*,' Tweedledee exclaimed, clapping his hands triumphantly. 'And if he left off dreaming about you, where do you suppose you'd be?'

'Where I am now, of course,' said Alice.

'Not you!' Tweedledee retorted contemptuosly. 'You'd be nowhere. Why, you're only a sort of think in his dream!...'

'I *am* real!' said Alice, and began to cry.

– from Alice Through the Looking Glass by Lewis Carroll (1832–98)

A Late Entrance

A dream that I have almost nightly is one of trying to arrive somewhere on time. I am constantly catching trains, taxis, aeroplanes. The destination might be a theatre, or it might just be a city that I am trying to reach. Always at the end of the dream I fail to arrive. It is then that I wake up in a state of some panic. This of course fits in with my ordinary life style, in that I present plays in some thirty countries, and in consequence am always haring around the world trying to catch up with myself.

– Derek Nimmo

Cemetery This spooky and emotion-laden location may be symbolic of something the dreamer would rather not remember, something preferably buried.

Being chased If it is the dreamer who is the quarry, this could indicate conflict between something both longed for and dreaded; if someone else is being chased, this could indicate the dreamer's unconscious antagonism towards the victim.

Child The child you see in your dreams quite often represents the childish side of your nature remaining though you may be an adult. By dreaming of yourself as a child without the inhibitions of adult status, you allow that side of your nature free rein; a child you do not quite recognise can also represent undeveloped aspects of yourself or a totally new situation to which you come as a figurative child.

Christ Like the other major religious figures, Christ can be a symbol of unachievable perfection as well as a way of life which may be aspired to, however imperfectly. If such religious figures appear to you in dreams, it may mean that there is a better way available than your life seems to offer at the time.

Church Like crosses and other religious symbols, the church may be figurative of the dreamer's idealism being surpressed, giving rise to conflict; desecrating a religious building may indicate that the dreamer fears that he may be breaking some religious taboo that he ought to respect. This is also a major symbolism for a place of safety and refuge.

Circle A significant image of wholeness and natural balance and may be understood to represent integration of the different aspects of personality.

City This may be a symbol of the dreamer's sense of social togetherness and his relationship to the community.

Climbing A common symbol for aspiration, the easier the climb the more natural the dreamer may find his efforts to succeed. If the dreamer feels that he could go on climbing into space or actually does so, it may be a sign that he relishes the danger of his waking situation.

Clock A ticking clock or the visualisation of seconds and minutes passing can indicate the dreamer's unconscious nagging him about a particular thing undone.

Clothes Representing as they do the facade the individual places between himself and the world, the clothing worn in dreams may reveal conflict between inner needs and external demands. If the dreamer is overdressed or wearing clothes which will not come off, this can be symbolic of overconforming to others' views and standards.

Clouds This can be taken as a symbol of the longing for escape from reality or a less arduous way out of a bad situation.

Colours Dream colours lend added import to the other images; the pace and variation of colour changes can indicate altered states of mind or mode.
  Black: the accepted colour of death and loss, it also suggests hidden aspects of life.
  Blue: a colour denoting spirituality and accepted images

Stage Fright

A recurring dream that I think quite a lot of actors share is that of going on stage and not remembering your lines. I wouldn't call it a dream — more of a nightmare. You walk out on to the stage, the house is full; they all have your attention, you open your mouth and nothing comes out; it's terrifying I can tell you. This usually happens the night before your first night of a play.

— J McArdle

'One can write, think and pray exclusively of others; dreams are all egocentric.'

— Evelyn Waugh (1903–66)

of otherworldly concerns.

Brown: an earthy tone suggesting basic concerns and growth.

Gold: the colour of the sun and also suggestive of wealth, golden hues can indicate a concern with the basic forces of life and prosperity.

Green: symbolises growth and fecundity as well as faith in the future and a hopeful disposition. On the other hand, a sickly, pallid green can have connotations of sickness and malaise.

Orange or saffron: an exotic hue suggesting unusual and unorthodox beliefs and ceremonies.

Pink: the colour of romance and illusion which may clothe reality and distort true meaning.

Purple: suggests strong and vibrant religious belief and subjugation of the individual to a higher force.

Red: basic, primal colour suggesting high emotions and dramatic confrontations with others.

White: can indicate a wish for a purer, cleaner life and relief from material pressures.

Yellow: a strong colour which can suggest impurity and staining apparently good intentions.

Corn Universal symbol of wealth and plenty; if stacks of corn are withering or burning, this can be a sign of fears of want and life slipping away.

Corridors with closed doors This can be taken as a strong image of missed opportunities and a confusion of possible directions and thwarted expectations.

'It was my eighth dream that I thought my tongue was so long that I wound it round the back of my neck, and forward into my mouth on the other side.'

— Thorstein's Saga (c.900 AD)

Cramped spaces This dream and attendant feelings of repression and frustration can mean that you feel some element of your life is closing in on you.

Crown A symbol suggesting victory or success in some endeavour close to your heart.

How a Broadcaster Deals with Dreams

There is a general assumption, I suppose, that dreams are entirely involuntary, that we have absolutely no control over them at all. Maybe eating pickled onions and strong cheese immediately before going to bed is not conducive to sweet dreams (at least not for your partner) but otherwise they come and go whether we like them or not.

I beg to differ.

I discovered many years ago that it IS possible to control dreams – at least in a negative sense.

When I was a youngster I made the mistake of going to see Dracula in the cinema. In those days they took their horror films seriously. No sending up. Dracula was a monster, and that was that. It worked, too, at least on impressionable ten-year-olds. I was utterly terrified.

When I finally managed to get to sleep that night I had the mother and father of a nightmare. Dracula's fangs slipped into my tender young throat with all the ease of my own teeth slipping into a choc ice in the Splott Cinema a few hours earlier. It was horrible. And it happened again. Night after night.

And then I read somewhere – probably the *Beano* – that the only way to deal with your fears was to confront them.

So when I went to bed that night and thought about Dracula, I actually TRIED to scare myself. I pictured him rising from his coffin in that dank cellar, and drawing back his lips in anticipation of his liquid lunch straight from the throat of some beautiful virgin. I pictured him gliding up the stairs of his castle and into the bedroom of the guest with the deepest cleavage. I pictured it all. The blood dripping down his chin, and the transformation of the youthful beauty into the un-dead – a bit like Doris Day becoming Joan Collins only worse.

It was horrible. I was terrified. And it worked.

I did NOT dream of Dracula. Then or since. So now, if I want NOT to dream of something, I think about it long and hard before I go to sleep. It never fails.

There is a problem, of course: I can't sleep because I'm so worried about what it is I'm so determined not to dream about.

But you can't have everything, can you?

– *John Humphrys*

D

Dancing This can indicate that you feel locked into a social situation or ritual with which you do not feel entirely comfortable; if you recognise the person with whom you are dancing, this could mean a wish for a closer connection.

Darkness Murkiness, a failure to see clearly certain elements of your dream could be a symbol for personal confusion and mixed emotions in your life.

Death In dreams, death does not always have the finality we associate with it in real life. It may simply be a dramatised indication of your negative feelings for someone or something in your life. If the deceased is yourself it may suggest that you are faced with something from which you would like to escape, and death is the ultimate escape.

Demon lover A common symbol, Jung thought, of the feminine side of the male personality and vice versa. A surrender to inevitable forces.

Depth If you find yourself seemingly sinking into unfamiliar territory it could be an effort of your unconscious mind to get to the bottom of some real-life puzzle.

Desert The familiar images of cactus, bleached bones, wide expanses of sand can suggest that you are less than satisfied with what you see as the aridity or bareness – emotional or physical – of your life.

Devil A cliché symbol for evil and menace and perhaps retribution which you may believe you deserve, this figure may represent the dangerous side of an important decision you feel that you must make. If the devil has a face you seem to recognise, this may indicate ambivalent feelings towards that individual.

Disfigurement This element in a dream could indicate lack of satisfaction with the justice of a decision you have made and the outward manifestation of feeling of inner ugliness.

Dragon Usually red, this is fairly established as a sex symbol suggesting a mixture of anticipation and fear of a new relationship.

Drama No matter what medium your dream takes place in – film, stage, television – this may indicate that you want to remove yourself from an emotional situation in which you feel uncomfortable. It may also be an

Mummy's Revenge

I was in Egypt in the Valley of the Kings. After visiting the tombs of Tutankhamen and Rameses II, I was told by my guide that another Pharaoh's tomb had recently been discovered, and if I was interested he would show it to me. I was delighted, as on a previous visit I had heard that archaeologists believed there was another tomb as yet undiscovered in that area. The entrance to the tomb was a short distance away, hidden behind a pile of rubble. As we approached it gaped darkly before us. The guide drew a torch from his pocket and motioned me to follow. We descended a long narrow shaft. The walls were covered with strange signs and hieroglyphics. We then reached a small chamber decorated with drawings of the dead Pharoh offering gifts to the Gods, surrounded by strange and beautiful birds and animals.

We then started to descend another, steeper shaft and soon came to a large, magnificently decorated chamber.

In the centre of the chamber was a huge stone sarcophagus guarded by four gilded statues. The lid of the sarcophagus had been removed to reveal another smaller coffin encrusted with gold and precious jewels. The guide slowly lifted the cover, and beneath it lay a heavily bandaged mummy. Round him in small earthenware jars were the necessities for his journey to the new life.

I was suffocating in the airless tomb, and although I was fascinated by what I was seeing, I was beginning to feel apprehensive, and unable to appreciate the excitement of this amazing discovery. As I stepped forward to get a closer view, a feeling of dizzyness overcame me and the mummy seemed to move. Suddenly to my horror it came alive, and bandages flying, it leaped out and grabbed me by the neck. Choking I heard a blood curdling scream dragged from my agonised throat. In the split second before I felt a sharp blow on the back of my head, and lost consciousness. I knew that there was no escape. I would be wrapped up and put in the mummy's place!

Happily, my own screams wakened me, and I decided, as relief flowed through my body, to give Egypt a miss on my next holiday, and never to eat Gorgonzola again before retiring!

— *The Dowager Countess of Dundonald*

Cat-and-Mouse

I have a recurring dream that I am in an old house under some threat. I am in the company of someone close and dear to me although this person appears to vary during the course of the dream. The approach of the unknown 'enemy' means the necessity to escape but I am not initially bothered because the house is riddled with secret passages known only to me. However, when it becomes necessary to depart I discover to my horror that the passages which I know from previous experiences to be navigable have become far too small to allow our egress. Even here to start with I am not especially worried as there are many variants available but all of them appear to have contracted and to be contracting as my panic rises.

There are others in the house who could help but none of them will listen to me; all of them explain that they are doing something more important, cooking etc. which they place, much to my anguish, above any needs of mine. Somewhere in the dream there tends to be a cat which suddenly attacks me and whose teeth and claws, although not particularly painful, I am unable to detach so I am forced to run about in my panic with this malevolent feline clinging to an arm or leg.

I wake always with immense relief to discover that none of this, although it appears extremely realistic at the time, has taken place.

– George Melly

effort to gain objectivity by becoming a spectator on your own life.

Dream within a dream This further removal from what you consider the realms of reality may indicate a refusal to accept the reality of a seemingly unresolvable situation.

Drinking May indicate an urge to get more out of life or drain some experience to the dregs. If the drink is spilled, this could mean that you feel some important experience is being spoiled by circumstances outside your control.

Dumbness If you try to speak in your dream but find that you cannot, this may denote a feeling of powerlessness and inability to communicate with the world.

E

Ears Any emphasis on the ears or hearing can be symbolic of a desire to know more of something about which you feel insecure or ill-informed. Conversely, if the dreamer hears everything too loudly, there could be an unconscious effort to be shielded from unwelcome facts.

Earth A safe image of comfort and protection from danger. However, if the earth seems to be endangered by external forces, this could reflect the dreamer's fear of hostility and uncertainty.

Being eaten Or being engulfed by some larger creature or force could be indicative that you feel involved in some bigger cause than yourself and consequently symbolically become part of that thing.

Eating A common dream image which can suggest a symbolic need rather than actual hunger. If the eating seems prolonged or seems to have no effect, this could be a sign of dissatisfaction with your emotional or intellectual life.

Egg A seminal symbol of the root source of life and human aspiration. But behind it lies the knowledge that without the outside element of fertilisation, the egg is sterile and will not develop. Perhaps a sign of an urge for inspiration or help.

Emotions It is very hard to gauge the validity of the emotions you may feel in your dream. They can often seem exaggerated or strangely muted, considering the elements of your dream. But they can be an accurate clue to your

---

God forbid that my worst enemy should ever have the nights and the sleeps that I have had, night after night – surprised by sleep, while I struggled to remain awake, starting up to bless my own loud screams that had awakened me – yea, dear friend! till my repeated night-yells had made me a nuisance in my own house. As I live and am a man, this is an unexaggerated tale –*my dreams become the substances of my life.*

– *Samuel Taylor Coleridge (1772–1834), romantic poet and critic*

unconscious attitude towards matters in your waking life.

Anger: perhaps against something which seems totally innocuous. This could mean that you are redirecting anger from one area of your life to another.

Anxiousness: one of the vaguest and most pervasive of dream emotions, this feeling could be so general and undirected as to be impossible to pinpoint on any particular element of your dream. It could even mean that the dreamer is anxious about any apparent lack of reason for anxiety in waking life. A careful examination of your life goals and the direction you are going could give you a clue.

Awe: a strong, almost religious feeling quite alien to your real-life attitudes and behaviour could indicate a lack of spirituality and an excess of rationalism in your life. This may be your unconscious telling you that you *need* to have something in your life toward which you feel wonder and respect.

Calm: unusual passivity and lack of concern, perhaps amidst seemingly disturbing dream images, could be a sign that you are fighting to repress strong emotions in your waking life.

Desire: strong pangs of desire, perhaps unmotivated by a particular dream, could be indicative of some long-buried

Greek Idyll

In my dream I found myself in a Greek Village Hall in the middle of a sunlit forest. The air was warm and still and no birds could be heard.

Inside the village hall a party was being given so the dead could meet the living. All the dead people looked perfectly normal, their clothes were casual 1950s, cardigans and slippers, rather like the clothes our grandparents wore. There were all ages there, from children to elderly, and they all looked alive.

The walls of the hall were a gloss cream colour. In the centre of the hall people were dancing in couples and children were running about, very happy, everyone was very happy.

Around the walls were tables covered in red crêpe paper, with drinks and nibbles on, some of the tables had nothing on.

In the dream I was observing the forest and the inside of the hall, I didn't feel I was a participant.

– Toyah Wilcox

Fairy Gold

A recurring dream I have had for many years involves an old bog – or moss as we would have called it in Ireland – which was located near my grandmother's house. It is an area where we used to play as children and collect the wild flowers that grew in that area where they cut the turf. But my dream is that I started to dig and find coins, and the more I dug, the more coins I found.

I don't know whether this was subconscious wishful thinking, but it's been there a long time!

– Gloria Hunniford

and seemingly forgotten feelings of love and desire fighting to the surface from your unconscious. This could also reflect your disappointment at the lack of this emotion in your waking life.

Fear: especially if exaggerated and all-encompassing, this emotion could indicate your hidden insecurity in some important area of life which you are trying to ignore.

Greed: if, in your dreams, you seem to have an insatiable desire for gain without apparent satisfaction, this could be a symbol for inner dissatisfaction in some area – emotional or material – or aspect of your life.

Hatred: especially random and poorly directed hatred towards either obscure, anonymous figures or the personification of people whom you love or respect can mean that you are not directing this emotion towards some person or organisation in waking life.

Indifference: like calm only stronger and more negative, this lack of emotion could mean that you are afraid to show strong emotions.

Enclosure If you are confined or imprisoned in your dream, try to examine closely the emotion this evokes. If you seem to accept it, this could indicate a need for boundaries which are lacking. If enclosure seems to create great distress, this could mean that you would like to fight against external restrictions but feel that you cannot.

Entanglement If something in your dream – the common images are ropes, cables, the tentacles of an octopus, vines, etc. – seems to hold you back or keep you in the path of some danger, this could indicate that you do not feel free to act against something which you feel has negative connotations for you. It could be something quite minor which your unconscious has magnified.

Escape Especially if you do not know quite what you are trying to escape from or if the escape route keeps shifting and changing, this urge and its frustration could indicate that you feel that you could avoid or get out of some life situation if only you had some external help. If in your dream a key to a door either doesn't work or will not fit in the lock, this could indicate that you feel you are being given bad advice.

Examinations or tests This dream can often allow rather than precede real-life hurdles of some kind which you may have cleared successfully. This could indicate

that you feel subconsciously that either you did not pass fairly or that the test was not a fair examination of your abilities.

Exchange If you are given something in exchange for something else in your dream – however unequal or ludicrous the objects (ie: gold or precious gems for some trivial object) – this could indicate that you feel that you are cheating or being cheated in some real-life exchange or negotiation.

Exhaustion If you seem very tired and drained of energy in your dream – possibly for no apparent reason – this could be a symbol for emotional rather than physical turmoil over some aspect of reality.

F

Failure A pervasive feeling of having failed, either at something concrete or in general, can reflect fear – even unrecognised – that you are unprepared for some major moral or intellectual test which you feel that you must pass.

Falling A classic dream image that is so common and so obviously an expression of insecurity that it is often dismissed as merely a symbol of fear of failure. However, falling should not be

taken too literally and must be considered as a metaphor for everyday anxiety, even about minor matters, which is exaggerated in the landscape of dreams.

False awakenings These frustrating phenomena when you seemingly awake only to find yourself still asleep and dreaming are common but difficult to interpret. It has been suggested that this is an indication that you are a person who feels a strong

> 'Human dreams do not easily forget old grudges.'
>
> *– Vladimir Nabokov (1899–1977), Russian-born American writer*

sense of mission or task which drives you to 'wake up' when the natural term of your dream has not yet passed.

Faltering A dream in which you seem to fall behind others in what may only marginally be conceived as a race or contest can be the unconscious expression of feeling that you are somehow 'behind' in a self-imposed schedule of accomplishment.

Family Familiar representations – literal or suggestive – of family members, some long deceased, often appear in dreams either with an ambiguous role or seeming to warn the dreamer of some impending misfortune. These figures can sometimes be taken as extensions of the dreamer's self and even represent opposing sides of the unconscious when the dreamer is trying to make an important decision. Often these images of family members have no other purpose than to assure the dreamer that he is 'not alone' and has behind him their support and comfort.

Fat If, in your dream, you are unaccountably fat or seem to be getting fat at an alarming rate, this could be a self-warning against letting material gains play too big a role in your life. In symbolism, fat can be taken as 'rich' in things rather than spiritual values. If, however, you are very fat in your dream and then suddenly become thin, this could be an image suggesting that you have 'given birth' to a new idea of conception.

Fences The meaning of the presence of fences in your dream is largely determined by your attitude and reaction to the fences; if they are somehow comforting and secure-making, they could reflect your need for security and support. If they are stifling and seem to be limiting your freedom, they could stand for elements in your life which you feel are standing between you and some goal.

Fields If idyllic or archetypal fields of plenty and peacefulness, these images can represent some yearned-for goal which you feel is as yet unattainable, however hard you strive towards it. If, on the other hand, the fields are distant and shadowy and may contain uncertain elements they could symbolise ambitions which you feel you should hold but about which you harbour uncertainties.

Fighting If the dreamer is fighting a known or familiar person or being, this may indicate the expression of hostility which cannot be admitted or expressed in everyday life. If, however, the foe is either anonymous, completely unknown or masked in darkness or secrecy, the dreamer is likely to be fighting some inner element which is thought to be a barrier to happiness.

I had a sort of dream-trance the other day, in which I saw my favourite trees step out and promenade up, down and around, very curiously – with a whisper from one, leading down as he pass'd me, *We do all this on the present occasion, exceptionally, just for you.*

– *Walt Whitman (1819–92), the American poet*

Fire This dream symbol encompasses the contradictory qualities of warmth and security and danger from without. To dream of a fire which somehow threatens – for no obvious reason – to get out of control is a sign that you may be frightened of the warmth of some human emotion going beyond heights with which you feel comfortable.

If, in your dream, you are trying to put out the fire with water, this could be an expression of your desire to 'throw cold water on' some enthusiasm or appetite which you feel may throw your life out of balance.

If, as opposed to a cosy, manageable fire, it seems to be everywhere and growing well out of control, this could represent a feeling that a great number of elements in your life – not all of them necessarily acknowledged – could be threatening your security.

Since fire is an important image for hell and punishment, a blaze which seems to both threaten and come from a mysterious source could be a way of expressing the fear of punishment for some real or imagined 'sin'.

If you are throwing things into the fire – especially things which are very valuable or dear to you – this could be your unconscious mind's way of warning you that some conscious behaviour is threatening things which you do or should value.

A fire which, unaccountably, neither burns things around it nor throws off heat, could symbolise a source of wisdom and understanding the light of which will increase your understanding of some perplexing mystery.

Flies If you or your food or some animal are unaccountably covered with flies which cannot be beaten off, this infestation could represent nagging doubts about the wisdom of some act which may have negative – if unforeseeable – consequences for you or those dear to you.

Food The presence of food in dreams, whether eaten or not, can represent nourishment of a completely non-material kind.

If the food seems unappetising, even artificial or waxen, this could indicate your doubt about the beneficial effects of some decision which, on the face of it, should bring profit to you.

If the food in your dream looks delicious but seems either tasteless or unpleasant this could be the expression of your ambivalence towards giving vent to other carnal appetites in your life.

If the food is over-abundant and very rich and filling or even slightly rotten, this could be an unconscious reaction to a situation which is giving you too much of a good thing or more than you bargained for.

A Bad Dream and a Good Dream

I have two recurring dreams, both very different and obviously tied up with my current situation and frame of mind.

The first is the typical actor's nightmare. I am about to do a live television show, and I am made up and dressed in a beautiful creation usually made of satin, with a long narrow hobble skirt. I am at the BBC Television centre and I'm trying to find my way to the studio, although I'm not sure where it is. I'm also not sure which show I'm doing or what I'm expected to do in the show. I keep telling myself that if the worst comes to the worst I'll make something up. As the dream unfolds it appears that the BBC is in the middle of major structural alterations. There is scaffolding everywhere, and new wet concrete on the corridor floors. I have to climb ladders and walk along duckboards desperately hampered by my night dress and high-heeled shoes. The TV Centre is a circular building. I wander round and round it like a mouse in a toy wheel, dodging gaping holes in the floor, leaping huge gaps in some cases, sidling past building equipment, my dress becoming more and more spattered, the hem so heavy I'm having to drag it along. I keep seeing clocks telling me that I am seconds from missing the programme. The workmen are polite and help me to manoeuvre my way through the obstacles, but none of them are able to enlighten me about where I should be going. My panic is painful. My heart beats and I sweat. The dream is never resolved. I just struggle on until I wake up.

My second recurring dream always leaves me feeling very relaxed and happy. I am at a small gathering of friends and relatives and we are enjoying the company and pleasant atmosphere. Suddenly I decide to push off with one foot and then I feel myself floating upwards towards the ceiling. With absolute ease and confidence I fly around the centre light, swooping and diving as gracefully as a swallow. I am totally elated and I call down to the others; "Look, I'm flying." They glance up for a moment, then carry on with their conversations as though nothing were happening.

People say I have this dream because I flew when I was playing 'Peter Pan', but that cannot be the case, for I have dreamt it ever since I was a small child.

— Wendy Craig

Staircase to Heaven

As a child, I was a bit disturbed to read somewhere that if you fell into a big space in a dream, such as off a cliff, you would die if you ever hit the bottom, and you had to wake up before you got there. One night I dreamt I was going along the upstairs landing of our house and I was just about to go downstairs when I thought to myself: Hold on, this is a dream, so you can jump from the top to the bottom without hurting yourself! A second later I realised that if I did that, I would also die. I hesitated a moment and then thought: Well, you'll never find out if you don't try. I jumped. I landed. I didn't die. In fact, it was so nice, I ran back upstairs and jumped again (at least twelve or fourteen steps – a huge jump for a small child) several times. After I woke up, I found I was still alive, so I actually had the dream again several times just for the sheer joy of the jump and soft landing. It was odd to think that I knew in my dream that I *was* dreaming, but I was still fast asleep. It was also odd that it never occurred to me to jump back upstairs as well. I always climbed up step by step.

– Miles Kington

Nightmare on the Air

During the War I acted in my spare time, when not at a De Havilland's drawing board. When the War ended I auditioned for the prestigious BBC Drama Repertory Company and was accepted. I was the rawest of recruits. I'd been to no drama school and had never broadcast before. I was welcomed warmly by everyone and shown great patience and courtesy. I was trusted at the beginning only with the smallest of parts, or playing two or three one-line parts in a long (or short) play or feature. I was surrounded by the best-known and most skilled radio actors in the land. I looked and listened and learned. And got paid for learning. I always looked forward to being in the radio-drama high point of the week, 'Saturday Night Theatre', often playing a fair-sized part – or more than one in the same play (I was a 'voices' feller). They were done live. You could go when you were done. You crept out.

A dream began, and went on for years and years, about 'Saturday Night Theatre'. I'd done my small part and left and was on my way home on the Tube, content. Suddenly I remembered with a *tremendous* shock I had another two lines. At the *end* of the normally quite long play! At the next stop I fought my way off the train through the (always packed) crowds trying to get on. On the other platform the wait for the train back seemed endless. At last it came. The stops back to Oxford Circus came slowly (the train *crawled*) and seemed to be *more* than usual. Again crowds (Saturday night – West End – everybody *happy*!) and I was the only one pushing against them. At last I was out, and running, breathless, staring-eyed.

As I reached the studio (top floor, long wait for lift, *slow* lift) the red light went out and the last members of the cast came out. They said goodnight perfectly normally. So did the producer and effects people. *Nobody mentioned the two lines. Ever.*

Then I would wake, utterly exhausted.

– David Kossoff

See back of book for dream forms and Dreamland blanket/duvet offer.

If the food on the table is so very strange that you can't recognise what it is and are afraid to eat it, this might be an image reflecting your rejection of a new or unfamiliar experience which is offered.

Forests Forests in a dreamscape are traditionally an invitation to adventure or freedom that other environments do not offer. They combine the danger of the unknown – once past the first line of trees – and the enjoyment of primitive life beyond the restrictions of the man-made. When you are in a forest in your dreams, you are deliberately placing yourself beyond civilisation and artificial restraints. If, however, you suddenly discover a house or other man-made structure amid the trees or precipitously come to the end of the seemingly endless forest, this can be an image for the reality that responsibility and constraints are never far away.

Fortune If you dream that you have suddenly come into a lot of money, this could be a representation of goals and ambitions to which you aspire but which you are not sure that you deserve.

Fossils (or bones) These could represent a former self which you have been trying to leave behind or deny. If these constantly turn up and are at one and the same time strangely familiar and repellent, it could mean that you are not being as successful at your 'new life' or disguise as you think.

Future Sometimes, for subtle or even obvious reasons, dreams seem to be set in some future time – either quite soon or away in the temporal distance. This could be the realisation of your wish that the present – which contains some unpleasantness or annoyance – should soon be over.

Dreams! My dreams are always disagreeable – mere confusion – losing my clothes and the like, nothing beautiful. The same dreams go on night after night for a long time. I am a *worse* man in my dreams than when awake – do cowardly acts, dream of being tried for a crime. I long ago came to the conclusion that my dreams are of no importance to me whatsoever.

— Thomas Carlyle (1795–1881),
Scottish historian and essayist

The Actor's Nightmare

Actors' dreams are very often to do with insecurity. A recurrent one of mine is that I seem to be preparing for the third act of *Charlie's Aunt*. It was always a difficult change of costume from day clothes into tails, especially as the starched collar and shirt front were so difficult to handle. The critical moment in the dream arrives when I can't find my trousers. We are being summoned to the stage and the others are getting anxious that I am not ready. 'You go on,' I say, 'I'll catch you up.' Over the speakers I hear the play progressing without me. In slow motion I continue searching for my trousers. Eventually I give up, get into my street clothes, and go down to the bus stop. As I am waiting for the bus, the rest of the company comes by in a car. They stop and, with a certain amount of justification, yell angrily at me 'Where were you!'. Then I wake up, usually in a cold sweat.

– Nigel Hawthorne

G

Gambling A natural assumption about a dream in which you were gambling would be to think that this related to a 'gamble' you faced in waking life. But in reality the act of gambling in a dream can indicate acceptance of the fact that all of life is a gamble in which certain natural rules apply and cannot be shaken. There is a tinge of fatalism to all gambling dreams whatever form they may take.

Games Here, too, the vehicle of games is a metaphor for life in that both require skill, enthusiasm, commitment, team play and a certain degree of specialisation and skill. More important than the individual form of game is the dreamer's degree of participation and commitment to the particular game about which he dreams.

Garden To dream that you are in a garden is quite different from dreaming that you *are* gardening. The former suggests enjoyment of conditions pre-set by others and beyond your control other than acceptance or rejection. The latter symbolises active involvement and creating one's own world accordingly to a plan in which one has a major influence.

Gates A universal symbol for access, gates can represent the way to a new phase or element of your life or work. The nature of the gates – elaborate, evocative of a style or era, weathered, etc. – can say much about the type of transition concerned, as can whether the gates are open or closed. A strongly locked set of gates can suggest difficulty in getting through to a new stage of your life.

Ghosts These symbolic representations can be the non-religious embodiment of the religious concepts of life after death, eternity, omniscience, rewards and punishments for our acts, etc. The dreamer who cannot believe in traditional religion and its rules can satisfy, at least in some way, the universal *need* to believe in something which is not bound by material rules. The behaviour of the ghosts in your dreams can be taken as a clue to what your unconscious is saying about your behaviour.

Giants These traditionally outsized creatures have to be seen in a different context from our everyday image of them. The dreamer may be seeing them from the perspective of a child and thus be accepting the giants in a quasi-

'A dream is a personal document, a letter to oneself.'

– Calvin Hall, Director, Institute of Dream Research

parental role. From this point of view the dreamer can better analyse the role of giants found in dreams.

Gifts As with gifts in waking life, perhaps the most important aspect of gift-giving is not the gift itself but the attitudes involved in both ends of the exchange. Though the gift itself may be significant, if the dreamer analyses carefully his attitude towards the giver (or vice-versa) a lot can be revealed about the significance of the act of giving and receiving in a dream context.

Goal Whether literally a sporting goal – such as soccer or rugby goalposts – or something more mystical which may not be seen very clearly but simply *seems* like a goal, this symbol for aspiration can indicate that you feel that some endeavour is growing close to completion and the goal may be reached soon. If the goal appears and disappears or seems unnecessarily far or difficult to get to, you may feel that you will not achieve your ends without further travail.

God When perceived in your dreams, a God-figure can be a

symbol for your father or other important male authority figure in your life. If the figure doesn't act very Godlike or seems to fail in some way, this could indicate a disenchantment with the authority figures in your life who seem to have let you down by being 'ungodly'. The dreamer also tends to use a Godlike posture as a yardstick for measuring all those who have a claim for respect and obedience.

Gold This is quite simply a symbol for value whether material or spiritual. The context in which you see the gold and the dream attitude toward it will have an important role in telling you the significance of the gold in your dream. If the gold is carelessly laid about or perhaps formed into something incongruous, it may indicate lack of respect and value, despite the image of gold, for the subject of your dream.

Grandparents Symbols of both respect and age, if your grandparents appear in your dream it may be a key to your desire for guidance and direction. It makes some difference whether they appear as *you* knew them (ie, quite old) or as you may have seen them in photos taken at an earlier time. But, either way, grandparents can be taken as clear figures of authority and direction and your desire for both. If they do not direct you in your dream, this may indicate that you really know what you must do and thus reject the influence of others, however much respected.

Grate The traditional fireplace grate in your dreams can be seen as a non-religious substitute for an altar or place of worship. As the resting place and source of fire, it is a site for reverence and awe but not of the conventional religious sort. Often the grate will be highly polished and shine like precious metal. This may reflect your need for a focus for religious feelings.

Groove (or rut) Finding yourself walking in a deep cut or groove in a road or landscape can strongly indicate that you feel locked into an unrewarding but difficult-to-escape situation, especially if, looking ahead, you can see no ending or outlets.

Guru (*see* GOD) This figure may be a God substitute if you find it particularly difficult to personify the godly.

Gypsy (or other travelling person) This person in your dream may represent the 'wild' side of your own nature and the loss of habit or inhibition you might long for but fear at the same time. Mark closely the behaviour of the gypsy and see how it relates to your own real or imaginary acts.

H

Habit A person or creature wearing a religious habit can stand literally for habits you either long to break or wish that you could establish and maintain. This is just one way that the unconscious mind fixes on a common association to reflect your own confusion or search for guidance.

Halter (or noose) A symbol both of duty and punishment. If you appear standing in a halter in your dream, this may symbolise either a feeling of guilt or a desire for more discipline despite your waking attitudes or feelings. Your attitude towards this sort of restraint can tell you a lot about its relevance to your life.

Handbag A symbol for both the maternal side of your nature and the source of undeserved gifts and benefits. If the handbag seems bottomless or to contain much more than its apparent size would indicate, this might symbolise your expectations of reward beyond your own merits.

Hands As one of the most expressive parts of the body, the hands very often serve as a clue to your attitude towards or connection with other elements in your dreams. If you are very conscious of your hands, it may mean that you feel totally responsible for some action which was 'by hand' but not necessarily under your control. If your hands seem to have a life of their own, this may tell you that you feel a lack of control for some things which you do. If your hands are very dirty or you seem keen to hide them, this may be a strong indication of guilt. If, in your dream, you are washing your hands, this is a common symbol for an expiation of guilt or an effort to absolve yourself for an act which, in your waking life, you may not acknowledge. If the hands are not yours and belong to

others or seem disembodied, they may represent outside forces urging you to act, especially if they seem to be trying to grab you or push you.

Hanging (execution) This image is not to be taken literally. Hanging (as well as other forms of execution) can be accepted as a symbol for either guilt or punishment – especially self-imposed – as well as deep-seated hostility. As with many dream metaphors, hanging serves as a substitute for other, less radical, expressions of feeling in that, in dreams, the individual is freed to express unconscious desires without fear of reproof.

Hanging (on) If in your dream you find yourself hanging onto or grabbing some person or thing, this may indicate your basic insecurity in some specific area and your need to cling. If your grip is broken, this may be your unconscious telling you that this desire is in vain.

Haven If you seek, or even more significantly find, what seems to be a place of safety and complete security in your dream, this may

'Dreams are true while they last, and do we not live in dreams?'

– Alfred, Lord Tennyson (1809–92), Poet Laureate

The Million-Pound Bike

When I was a child I had a recurring nightmare, it generally happened when I was feverish. It still stands out in my memory because it was so vivid and, at the time, so awful, yet on the surface seems to be rather ridiculous. However, it was very real at the time.

I would be offered a gleaming sports car or a yacht or a motorcycle for a penny and would rush to buy it. Having agreed on the purchase and ready to hand over my penny I was told that I'd made a mistake, that it was actually £1,000,000 and I was forced to buy it! What an analyst would make of this I don't know but, like Hermione Gingold and Maurice Cheavalier in *Gigi*, 'I remember it well'.

– David Jacobs

mean that in your working life you feel a 'danger' from some element beyond your control. This danger need not be literal, but in dream terms you are allowed to give it an importance which it may not deserve.

Heat This symbol for passion or emotion may have many sources in your dream or none which is obvious to you, but it may indicate that you are uncomfortable with the degree of involvement which has developed with another. If you find that you are becoming comfortable with the heat or it suddenly lessens, this could be a sign that the emotion is beginning to fade. Unbearable heat can also be a symbol for guilt or feeling that you deserve punishment.

Help If you find yourself seeking help in a dream – even if you do not know what for – it's a pretty safe bet that you are less than sure or satisfied with some aspect of your life and deep down feel that you could be doing better. If it is you who are giving help to others, you may feel that you are overburdened by the demands of others.

Hole (or chasm) Often in our dreams we find ourself faced with or looking down into a hole or fissure in the ground. Sometimes this may seem to be bottomless. The key to the meaning of this

symbol is your attitude towards it. Alternatives could include: satisfaction because this is a place to hide things you do not want seen; or trepidation because the hole seems a pitfall which could trap you.

Home The ultimate security symbol and very easy to distinguish from a mere dwelling or habitation (*see* **House**) by the emotion attached to this unique place. To dream frequently of going home – often to a house remembered from the distant past and not too realistically – is a way of expressing the need for the safety and warmth inherent in such a place.

Hospital An attractive/repellent image which at one and the same time offers both help and potential pain and suffering. This can be a symbol for ambivalent feelings about some new venture or experience.

House As in waking life, houses in your dreams convey a multitude of emotions. As with many common symbols, the house can represent the dreamer and his attitude towards other elements in the dream. For instance:

A familiar house filled with strangers can suggest that you are not receiving the love and regard to which you feel entitled.

A house in poor repair could

indicate fears for some aspect of your health.

A house which is like a film set, all front and no interior, might signify fears that you are putting up a false image to the world.

A house in which you feel ill at ease could relate to a role in your waking life with which you are not comfortable.

A house where refurbishment always seems to be going on could indicate your desire to improve yourself in some regard.

Hunger Generally an indication of some emotional or sensual gap, real or imagined, in your life.

Bush Child Dream

The sun's riding low in the morning acacia: it's not quite turned 6 am.

The elephants are crossing the Luangwa, silently and the morning's cool as a dream.

The crocodiles are warming on the sand bars downstream of the Mfuwe bridge. The hippos are returning to the water.

Cautious for the lions I know are not far off – I saw their evening kill a mile back, a half-buffalo beneath a baobab – I don't see him till I meet him.

He's nine or so and black (my daughter's six and blonde); he's wearing starched blue shorts and a t-shirt some wildlife photographer's cast off has left behind – its motto states "Support my Right to Arm Bears..."

I greet this lad and he me. We pass in the bush. I gaze down on the dual time panel of my everything-proof Casio, thinking of my daughter getting up this moment, 5000 miles north, considering her schoolday, as he is considering his schoolday.

I think then of their futures and am suddenly scared for him. And her. She can't yet tell the time, reads with difficulty...he is walking in the direction of the lion's kill. I call out – *mkango* in Chinyanja. He stops, hears, waves, shouts back pointing to the path. And goes on.

That night, in my *banda*, the geckos clicking in the thatch and the night wild with possibilities, in those jungled moments of half-sleep: it's then I love my daughter and this small man of Africa, striding off to class along a bush path, firm enough to face any challenge time may chuck at him – his sums, his letters and the lions roaring me to sleep.

– Martin Booth

Daydreaming

There's plenty of time both to dream and day dream whilst climbing Himalayan mountains. This was certainly the case when, on our expedition in 1981, we were caught by a savage storm high on Mount Kongur, a mountain of 7719 metres in China. We were trapped in a tiny snow cave for three days and four nights.

The place where we dug our snow cave had only three feet of snow before hitting hard ice. As a result we could only dig a narrow tunnel in which we could barely sit up and in which it was difficult to communicate with each other. There was a very high level of sensory deprivation since inside the snow hole there is no sound at all as the scream of the wind is deadened by the snow. During the day there is a flat, even light that is filtered through the thin snow wall. We had nothing to read and very little to eat. The day was measured by cooking the daily meal and having the occasional brew from melted snow. For the rest of the time we just lay in our sleeping bags dozing and contemplating the light patterns on the sculpted snow a few inches above our noses.

Daydreaming and dreaming slid into each other. I became obsessed with food, or to be more exact, with breakfasts. At home I very rarely have more than a couple of rounds of wholemeal toast but I've always loved the traditional English breakfast and I found myself daydreaming about colossal breakfasts – bacon, sausage, black pudding, fried kidneys, fried bread, fried banana, fried tomatoes, fried eggs (easy under). I could hear them sizzling in the frying pan and smell that bacon and eggs frying smell and, through that, was transported home to our big kitchen.

Dreams of breakfast took me through three and a half days of waiting for a break in the weather and then, at last, it cleared and we were able to go for the summit of Kongur.

– *Chris Bonington*

See back of book for dream forms and Dreamland blanket/duvet offer.

I

Ideal If something in your dream seems to be absolutely perfect, just the thing or person you have always been looking for, this could indicate that in your waking life you are setting standards in some regard which are so high that they are not likely to be attained. You might reassess these standards to see if you are not trying to avoid that thing or person rather than seeking the best or most suitable.

Illness As the patient in your own dream you could be looking for attention you are being denied and which almost always goes to the ill. This could also be a reflection of your need for more sympathy and understanding and a sign that you want to be treated as a 'special case'. If it is others in your dreams who are ill, this could symbolise your feeling that too many demands are being made on you by friends and associates. Repeated dreams that you are ill could be your unconscious way of excusing yourself from unwelcome or overwhelming demands which are being put upon you.

Insects There are probably as many symbolic possibilities for the insects you dream about as there are insects. In general, they may be said to represent some thing or situation which is at the same time insignificant and annoying or uncomfortable. Some of the symbolic meanings of specific insects include:

Ants: can be images reflecting your attitude towards either work or discipline and the need to subordinate your individuality to the will of the group.

Bees: symbols of both reward (honey) and pain (stings) which can come from the same situation or experience.

Beetles: representations of both dirt and decay, possibly hidden decay or the insidious effect of aging. Fear of growing or being considered old though you may still feel young.

Butterflies: symbols of simultaneous beauty and vulnerability or shortness of life. A suggestion that you don't take life as seriously as you should.

Gnats: could represent annoyances which you know you should be above but which nonetheless bother you.

Moths: a symbol of decay, often not obvious but discovered upon close examination. Could be a metaphor for the futility of the trappings of wealth and their ultimate destruction.

Spiders: a symbol of both predation and construction with

definite overtones of fear of being trapped. Not always a negative image, but one with strong emotional connotations.

Intruder This generally menacing symbol could reflect the dreamer's fear of alien encroachment into his private area. If the intruder is recognisable – however ludicrous this may seem – you could be expressing fear of others intruding into what you consider your personal domain. If the intruder is faceless or unknown to you, this may represent a feeling of not knowing clearly who your friends and enemies are. If you seem to welcome – rather than fear or resent – the intruder, this could be a sign that you lack the unknown element of adventure in your life.

Intuition If you find – or imagine you find – that you seem to be able to resolve problems in your dream through some force of intuition, this could suggest that you feel particularly baffled by some aspect of your waking life.

Invisibility If you are seemingly invisible in your dream, that you can walk among the dream population apparently unnoticed, this may be an indication that in some real-life situation you feel under particularly close scrutiny or investigation and wish that you

> One night I dreamed I was a butterfly, fluttering hither thither, content with my lot. Suddenly I awoke and I was Chuang-tzu again. Who am I in reality? A butterfly dreaming that I am Chuang-tzu or Chuang-tzu imagining he is a butterfly?
>
> *– Chuang-tzu*
> *(3rd century BC)* .

had the power to escape this attention. If it is others in your dream who become invisible, this may mean that you feel it is difficult to get past the façades of those around you. You may feel isolated by your failure to feel that you really get to know those around you.

Irrigation Dreams featuring green fields or pastures obviously being irrigated could indicate your feeling that you exist in an artificial situation in which personal growth is not possible by 'natural' means. If the apparatus of irrigation – channels, hoses, sprinklers, etc. – are present but no water is apparent, this could express your fear that some situation or relationship could 'wither and die' through some means beyond your control.

Early Warning

My partner Terence Brady has spent most of his life resolutely refusing to fly in aeroplanes, let alone helicopters. Imagine then how we laughed when I awoke one night from a terrifying dream that we were flying in a helicopter over New York and the helicopter was nosediving towards the thin line of the Hudson while the pilot shouted, 'I can't hold this thing!' Some hope of US finding ourselves in such a situation, we thought to ourselves.

Three months later we were summoned to Hollywood to write a series. We stopped off in New York during a snowstorm. The service included a helicopter straight into the centre. Forgetting my dream, I clambered aboard with my petrified partner who'd spent most of the flight in the loo. It wasn't until I saw that thin ribbon of water below us that I remembered my dream — too late. And then, hearing the pilot shouting 'I can't hold this thing!' I turned ashen-faced to my partner and said, 'Oh my God my dream…' This time however I had no need to wake up, the helicopter's landing would have jolted the unconscious awake. This time too no-one laughed. Everyone who took that flight and landed safely shook hands and said, 'never again…!' For myself, I am only glad I don't dream too often, I might find it difficult to get out of bed in the morning for fear of having such an experience again. We read of dreams coming to us as warnings, but until that moment I have to say I thought the idea a little fantastical.

– Charlotte Bingham

Island A strong symbol representing both security and isolation, perhaps the contradiction of these two qualities in your life. In a sense, you *are* the island and its occupant if any. Your dream attitude towards being on the island and the others you find there – if you are not alone – will say a lot about your feelings about your relationships with those most close to you.

See back of book for dream forms and Dreamland blanket/duvet offer.

The Big Hit

I actually dream quite a lot but rarely remember them for long.

One thing I must confess to though is being a compulsive day dreamer. I day dream in the car on motorways, often whilst listening to music, but not always. I tend to dream up plays or musicals, books or films, even television series. Whole creative works, which are all certain box offfice smash hits, until the end of the motorway, when they evaporate. I once wrote a West End full scale muscial, complete with a harbour set, and ship, which converted into a monastery and village square before the amazed audience. It was stunning and would run for as long as *The Mousetrap*, if only I could remember the plot and the tunes.

One of my biggest, imaginary, hits was a completely innovative form of chat show. So revolutionary and inventive was it that I decided I must write it down at the next service station. So some fifteen minutes later I pulled into Watford Gap, only to realise that, by then, I was halfway through creating a spy novel and busting to know who the double agent was, and who was trying to get at the hero's dead letterbox. So of course I had to continue my journey and another great first in British Broadcasting was lost to the world.

What fascinates me though is this; are others doing it? As I wend my way down the M6 or crawl around the M25, is the driver of the Volvo, in front of me halfway through a new version of *Last of the Summer Wine*? Is that Montego speeding past full of a never-to-be-seen Space adventure? Are the lanes alive to the sound of unwritten masterpieces destined to evaporate in a contraflow somewhere up the M62? Quite a thought, isn't it? Britain's highways and byways bursting with unrecognised Harold Pinters and unsung Lloyd Webbers.

I once took a dictation machine with me to try and capture, for the sake of posterity, one of my transient masterpieces. Of course nothing came to me, absolutely nothing. I didn't take it again. Well, motorway driving is boring enough and who wants to be deprived of some of the greatest works never heard by man?

Sweet dreams!

– Christopher Lillicrap

J

Jars (or other glass containers) These can symbolise your need to both preserve and compartmentalise the various aspects (emotions particularly) in your life. This may indicate that you feel that you are mixing up things which ought to be kept separate. Aside from the impracticality of this desire, it is well to be aware that things in jars are invariably sterile, dried or dead, and this may express your need to make safe 'dangerous' elements in your life by keeping them apart.

Jewels Often these represent something at the same time valuable and rare and remote from everyday life. When, through whatever means, jewels in your dreams are seen to symbolise or represent individuals in your life, this could refer to the precious qualities of virtue, value, purity and incorruptibility with which you invest them. If, however, what seems to be a jewel from a distance turns out, on closer inspection, to be fake, this could indicate your disillusionment

---

I dreamt last night that I had a disease of the heart that would kill me in six months. Leonard [her husband], after some persuasion, told me. My instincts were all such as I should have, in order, and some very strong: quite unexpected, I mean volunatary, as they are in dreams, and thus have an authenticity which makes an immense, and pervading impression. First, relief – well I've done with this life anyhow (I was lying in bed) then horror; then desire to live; then fear of insanity; then (no this came earlier) regret about my writing, and leaving this book unfinished; then a luxurious dwelling upon my friends' sorrow; then a sense of death and being done with at my age; then telling Leonard that he must marry again; seeing our life together; and facing the conviction of going, when other people went on living.

– Virginia Woolf (1882–1942), novelist and critic,
her diary entry for 2 November 1929

with someone or something close to you who has not lived up to your high standards or expectations.

Various specific jewels:

Crystal: a symbol for purity and the refraction of light, it can also have connotations of the balance of perfect qualities.

Diamond: often a symbol of hardness and perfect symmetry more brilliant than warm. An overabundance of diamonds could indicate a desire to dazzle rather than impress with more human qualities.

Pearl: symbolic both of wholeness and mythic knowledge.

Ruby (including garnets and other red stones): symbolic of sacrifice and bloodshed and – illuminated by light behind – shedding a reddish tint of passion and dramatic illumination on some situation.

Sapphire: this stone suggests coolness rather than warmth; its blueness symbolises watery depths which may take you beyond the realms with which you can cope.

Journey (or travelling) Almost any dream journey can be taken as a reflection of some aspect of your passage through life. The conditions of the journey – easy or hard, exciting or boring, promising or depressing – can relate to some aspect of your life,

> The Huron indians of Eastern America believe that dreams brought on by fasting give them the power to see the invisible world.

conscious or unconscious.

Vehicles: these, of course, vary widely and can symbolise the nature and quality of the portion of your life involved:

Aeroplanes lend feelings of high-flying exhilaration and flights of imaginative passages over the heads of the ordinary, but also convey basic insecurity and the possibility of a sudden disaster. Risk-taking – whether voluntary or forced – is implicit in this dream.

Balloons have some of the high-flying associations of aeroplanes but suggest a loftier, quieter, less destination-oriented passage with higher ethereal qualities borne on the wind rather than rushing through it.

Bicycles are the symbolic transportation of childhood and youth. If the bicycle is too large or too small, this can indicate your degree of self-perceived readiness for a particular aspect of life's journey.

Boats convey the mystery of the long voyage with an uncertain goal. They – especially submarines – suggest the possibility of depths to be plumbed before the voyage (and further enlightenment) is completed. Submarines suggest as well that you are not content to examine the surface of things but must delve into their depths in search of the solution of mysteries.

Buses are a commonplace and prosaic means of travel which may indicate that you are content to sacrifice more dramatic and glamorous ways and accept less excitement for more security and sureness.

Cars connote a relatively swift and smooth passage but one still earthbound and subject to earthly realities such as other traffic, the availability and cost of fuel and the necessity of having roads.

Motorcycles are almost universally connected with youth, rebellion and danger, especially if you are not yourself the driver and thus have no direct control over what could be a wild and dangerous ride.

Trains could indicate that you feel you have a powerful, directed aim in life but also that you accept the limitations of freedom that rails indicate.

Driver (or captain or pilot): if you recognise the person in charge of the journey, it may indicate that this is someone to whom you are willing to give your trust. If the journey then goes wrong, it could suggest that you feel your trust has been misplaced. If *you* are the driver, this could represent your desire to take command of and direct your own life and its direction.

Night journeys or voyages with obscured or curtained windows indicate your uncertainty as to just where the journey of life is taking you at this particular moment.

An Opera Singer's Dream

Val Hennessy of YOU magazine asked Pavarotti to describe an opera star's worst nightmare. Interpreting the question literally he replies, 'My worst nightmare I dream I am wearing only my underpants and pom-te-pom-te-pom the overture plays, the curtain goes up and I am on stage wearing only my underpants.'

After a solemn pause he continues, 'It nearly happens once in Paris. Half an hour before I am ready the music starts playing and I am shouting, "Stop! I am only in my underpants! Delay the performance."'

– *Pavarotti*

Running can indicate a streak of self-reliance and acceptance that you must be responsible for the length and direction of life's journey and accept both pain and sacrifice.

Walking, like running, indicates self-reliance and an eagerness to set your own pace in life. But, unlike running, it indicates a willingness to take your time and not rush into things. Unlike the runner, you are not so much concerned with the goal as with the experience itself.

Destinations: if your destination seems certain or is clearly indicated by internal evidence in the dream, it could mean that you feel secure in this part of life's journey. If your destination is uncertain, your attitude towards this mystery could indicate your general attitude towards the uncertainties of life. If a listed destination is proved to be wrong, you may feel that your life is taking an unpleasant or uncertain turn.

Judge If you dream of a judge or other authority figure who is responsible for handing down decisions, it could mean that you feel that you are on trial in some aspect of your life. The seeming attitude of the judge towards you or some other person in your dream could be a clue to your attitude towards receiving justice in your life.

Juggling Symbolic for balancing disparate elements or activities which may or may not conflict. If you are the juggler, it could mean that you feel personal responsibility for a particularly complicated course of action. If you are juggling well (or badly), this could be your own judgement of how well you are succeeding. Juggling with fire or sharp or dangerous objects could symbolise chances you feel you are taking.

Juice Could represent the essence of some experience from which you feel you are deriving some basic understanding of life.

The Roman Emperor Domitian [51–96 AD] dreamed the night before he was slain that a golden head was growing out of the nape of his neck; and indeed, the succesion that followed him, for many years, made golden times.

– from *Of Prophecies by Sir Francis Bacon (1561–1626)
philosopher and statesman*

K

Karma If you feel that everything in your dream is somehow ordained, taking a predestined course, this may suggest an inner wish for external control on elements of your life which you feel are too anarchic and random.

Key This is a traditional symbol for an answer or solution to a problem or puzzle. If in your dream you hold or find a key, this may indicate that you sense that some clue to a solution is within your reach. If you seek, but cannot find, a key which you expected to be there, it may mean that your struggle towards knowledge or enlightenment is ongoing. If there is no key or the key does not fit, this could indicate that you feel that there is no real solution to a particular problem.

Kindling a fire In your dream this seemingly simple act could be a symbol for seeking inspiration in some endeavour or other. The 'fire' you are kindling could be a creative act which you feel you need to begin.

King This strongly symbolic character can stand for almost any authority figure in your life, especially one who you feel is due great respect, even reverence. More important, perhaps, than which specific person the king figure is supposed to represent is *your* attitude towards him and, less important, your apparent relationship with him in your dream.

Kismet Much like **Karma**, this feeling of surrender to forces much stronger and greater and more compelling than your own could indicate a wish on your part to stop struggling and flow with life forces towards some pre-set destiny.

According to Lady Dorothy Carrington, the writer, now living in Corsica: 'On the island of Corsica, whole villages have collective dreams. The Corsican belief is that if you kill an animal in your dream and recognise it as a person in your village, that person will die.'

Kissing This act, usually considered affectionate or romantic, could instead symbolise the transfer of energy or life forces from one being to another. If, in your dream, you find yourself kissing someone repellent or someone from your waking life

Wishful Thinking

Not surprisingly my dreams are often about sport. One dream recurs frequently.

I am at Wembley for the Cup Final, one of 100,000 people. We sing 'Abide with Me' and no-one tries to drown us out. There are no arrests for drunken or disorderly behaviour and when a player scores, his mates do not come up and kiss him.

Suddenly, I am at Lord's for the Test, a bowler takes a wicket and he does not punch the air in glee. He seems to think he's only doing what he should be doing. No-one in the crowd taps out a tattoo on a beer can.

Why am I now sitting ringside? I have no idea, but it occurs to me that there are only eight world champions, instead of 40-odd, and most of us know who they are. And what's this? The fighters are coming into the ring without a legion of semi-naked girls surrounding them and we are not being deafened by raucous rock.

This is a very strange dream, because now I'm at Putney for the Boat Race and the crews are rowing without trying to cut each other up.

And I'm sitting at Wimbledon where players accept line-calls without dispute and no-one is shrieking obscenities at the umpire.

– Harry Carpenter

whom you would not likely feel affection for, it may indicate that you feel that you could gain something spiritual from that person. A kiss which can't be broken away from may symbolise a relationship you can't seem to bring to an end.

Kite The kite which flies high is still a prisoner of the earth and the being flying it. This symbol could indicate that you feel bound to another and kept both from your ultimate goal and – this may be paradoxical – from the dangers of complete freedom. If you identify with the kite flier and not the kite, you may feel in danger of losing someone about whom you do not feel very secure.

Knight A figure strongly suggestive of your most altruistic and noble insticts. How the knight in your dream fares may indicate your own ambivalent attitude towards the way you behave and the way you think you should behave. If the knight is in clean and shining armour, you may feel that you are keeping up a certain level of behaviour. If he is low and dirty or defeated in battle, this could represent your own sense of failure.

L

Laboratory This familiar image could very well represent an environment in which you feel that you can safely experiment and test certain attitudes or positions which in another place might well be dangerous. If an experiment in your dream is a success, this may mean that you feel that you have tried something in a controlled – and therefore safe – environment and now could try it elsewhere. If an experiment in your dream laboratory fails or even explodes, it could mean that you do not yet feel confident enough to make some (possibly important) 'experiment' in your life.

Lad (or boy) There's a very good chance that this figure represents yourself even if you are female. The small boy is such a classic symbol of inexperience and youthful endeavour that it transcends gender. How this figure reacts to or overcomes conditions in your dream could be a clue about your own feelings towards the challenges you face in your life.

Ladder An obvious metaphor for progress or transition from one stage to another, a ladder can represent your own unconscious feeling towards some important step in your life. If the ladder seems unusually tall or daunting, this could indicate your reluctance to 'step out' on some venture or other. If the ladder is especially frail or broken, this could mean that you doubt the soundness of wisdom of some undertaking on which you may be about to embark. If the ladder seems to have unusual properties – growing longer ahead of you or disappearing behind you – this could symbolise your fear of committing yourself and not being able to 'climb down again.

Lame If you or another central figure in your dream is lame or finds it difficult to walk properly, this could indicate your lack of confidence in your ability to carry through some activity or procedure you are about to undertake. If you find that the foot or leg in which you are lame keeps changing, it may indicate that you don't fully trust your own judgement in some matter and are looking for an excuse to back out of a commitment.

Languages The languages which make up the atmosphere of your dream can tell you a lot about your own confidence in your understanding of the world in which you find yourself in life. If the language is peculiarly difficult – or even nonsense – but you seem to understand it easily and even speak it, this could mean that you feel competent beyond the demands put upon you. But if you feel completely baffled – or even confused and worried – by a language with which you just cannot come to grips, this could translate as a lack of confidence to succeed at a given role or task.

Letter This vehicle for communication can indicate that you are waiting for understanding of some sort which may or may not reveal a mystery. The letter often represents the unknown, the surprise element in life, the opening up of oneself even to 'bad news'. If you find that your letter is especially difficult – or even impossible – to open, this may indicate that you are not yet ready for some revelation. If the letter is already open, you may feel that someone has deprived you of the right to discover for yourself an important truth. If on opening the letter you find that it is very distorted or unclear for any reason, this could mean that you lack the background or maturity of understanding fully to comprehend some difficult concept which is trying to be revealed to you.

Lichen To find a tree, rock or other object covered with lichen or moss could indicate your willingness to be patient in waiting for some important development.

Lift An image pertaining to success and failure. If the lift is taking you up, this could indicate that you feel on the right track. If down, this could mean you doubt the wisdom of some course of action. If the lift seems to plunge, you may know unconsciously that you need to make a serious change.

Light A very important symbol of knowledge, intuition, understanding and truth, this image can come in a wide variety of common and more esoteric forms. Perhaps the most important thing is not the source but just how much the light enables you to see and understand around you. If the light markedly improves your perception of your dream environment, illuminating even the furthest reaches and corners, this could indicate that you feel confident that at last you are beginning to understand something which has been confusing you. If the light is weak or intermittent or fails just as it seems about to reveal all, this could mean that you are waiting to learn more about something before taking a risk or gamble.

Lighthouse This symbol of safety and security can be seen as a safeguard which stands ready to protect the dreamer from dangers which lurk in the dark. The stronger the light, the more you may feel protected against unexpected menace. However, if the lighthouse is dark, this could be a symbol that an expected source of insight and security has failed you.

Lightning Lightning threatens as well as illuminates. Thus it may stand as a symbol of knowledge which may somehow be dangerous or forbidden. If you dream that a bolt of lightning strikes close by but does not harm you, this could indicate that you realise that some imagined danger is not really a threat to you. If the lightning is general – such as so-called sheet lightning – rather than intense and localised, this might indicate knowledge that there is potential danger all around but not specifically aimed at yourself.

Lips If you dream that your lips are unable to open or even no longer there, this could mean that you feel in danger of revealing a confidence and need support from some outside force to keep it.

Barrage Balloons

When I was a child in World War II, one of the most electrifying and frankly terrifying experiences of my life was seeing the first barrage balloons over my home town of Hull.

I still have dreams of menacing balloons hanging in the sky and can actually go into daydreams sitting in a car, say at traffic lights, watching advertising bills or even jet planes over London. I always see them as 'hung' in the sky and I cannot explain why they give me the creeps.

Still, I have flown nearly everywhere in the world so it seems I am all right so long as I am thousands of feet up there inside my dream!

— *Jean Rook*

Liquor If you find yourself drinking intoxicating spirits in your dream – whether or not it has any effect on you – this may indicate a desire to escape from some fact or reality or element in your life with which you feel unable to cope.

Loss An acute or long-lasting sense of unexplained loss in your dream could indicate that you feel a lack of direction and are unconsciously searching for something which could indicate some future course of action. If you seem actually to have lost something in your dream but simply cannot find it, the key may be in the objects which you find and disregard. One of them may be the lost item which is simply not recognised. This may indicate

a certain confusion in your life about making the right choices and your faith in your ability to make the right decision on important matters.

Luck If you find that you are gambling and winning time after time, this might be a sign that you feel that you are ready to take some big step in your life that others will consider a serious gamble.

Lust Acute feelings of sexual feeling in your dreams may indicate that you are feeling the need to repress such feeling in your waking life. This is especially true if the emotion is very strong and not seemingly directed at any one person.

M

Machinery A dream that you are surrounded – or even engulfed – by machines of any sort could indicate that you feel caught up in some enterprise in which you feel less than independent and free to act as you want to. Once again, the meaning of your dream will depend to a degree on your attitude towards your environment. If you seem very happy in your dream, the machine *could* be a symbol of security and protection.

Madness If you or someone else in your dream behaves in some of the ways we traditionally associate with madness, this could symbolise a reaction to pressures on you to conform to a constricting norm in some part of your life from which you feel impelled to break away through unorthodox behaviour.

Market A common symbol for an environment of give-and-take and commercial activity which could represent your feelings that you are gaining control over your life and beginning to behave in a 'free market' manner which enables you to control your own life.

Marriage This ritual – the more conventional and dressed in archetypal trappings – could likely symbolise not a literal marriage but your own feelings that you are being permanently committed ('til death do us part') to some course of action or behaviour. Your true feelings towards this could, of course, range widely. If the unexpected or bizarre intrudes on the ceremony, this could be a sign of stifled rebellion.

Mask A mask in your dreams is a common mode of expressing either the need to hide behind social conventions or to break free of some role which you feel is being imposed on you. If you can't take the mask off or become uncertain whether you *are* wearing a mask, this could symbolise discomfort and confusion over some part you are being asked to assume. If the mask you or another wears is the face of another about whom you feel strong emotion or even aggression, this could indicate your fear to express yourself to the actual person.

Matter (changing) A dream in which the usual fabric of life seems either to change beyond your control or be constructed of unusual materials clearly indicates a degree of uncertainty and insecurity in a new and unfamiliar environment.

A Dream I Would Like To Have

I was walking home from work along a London Street when I heard a scream. I stopped to see who was making the noise. Suddenly I saw a man with a knife holding a girl hostage. I slipped down the alley and started to fight him. When he started to run away I tripped him up and he almost stabbed himself. I pulled my tie off and tied him up. Then I called the Police and they identified him as John Streak and said he had committed four murders and there was a reward of £100,000. The next day I was in the paper and decided to retire.

Timothy Beaujeux
Shiplake Primary School
Age 11

Meeting If you attend a meeting, especially of strangers who seem indifferent or hostile to you or even threaten violence, this could indicate that you feel unsure of some support which you may have taken for granted. If, on the other hand, you feel from that gathering a sense of support or even affection, this is a sign that you are feeling at home in some environment.

Mill This is a standard symbol for the transmutation of matter from one form to another and may indicate that you feel that you are undergoing a process of change which may literally turn you into something which you are not. If you feel that you are trapped or caught up in a mill, this could indicate that you feel threatened by the process.

Mirrors The most important part of the mirror symbol is what it reflects. If you are surrounded by mirrors and they present to you an image which is radically different from what you expect to see, this could indicate that you are unsure of the image you are expected to present to the world or that someone is expecting an image – or behaviour – of you which is unnatural. The archetypal 'funhouse' mirror which grotesquely distorts your image in some way may suggest that you are being distorted by forces from outside. A cracked or hazy mirror could suggest concern about aging or the passage of time without accomplishment. One-way mirrors suggest that you feel under close observation, possibly of a critical or hostile nature.

Mist (or fog) This is an image representing confusion with some function or role which you are expected to fulfil in life. If in the mist you seem to find a clear path, this could represent either the beginnings of a way out of some confusion or the wish for the same. If the mist clears in response to a strong external source of light, this could indicate that you feel someone – possibly someone new – could help you find the way you are looking for.

Mixing If in your dream you find yourself or another mixing various ingredients either in a kitchen environment or possibly a cement mixer, this might indicate that you are trying to put together the 'right' elements to solve some problem. If the ingredients you are mixing are ludicrous or clearly unsuitable, this could symbolise your feeling that what you are trying to accomplish is impossible or against your own interests.

Monastery (or nunnery) This image with its strongly identifiable symbols of robes, habits, strong walls and stringent rules, could indicate that you feel

---

The Peasant's Dream

It was only now, after arriving at the Pian del Sotto, that I had begun to dream. I started to dream on the first night, and every succeeding night I dreamt the same dream: that I was picking up stones on the Pian del Sotto and it seemed to me that it lasted most of the night. The only time when I was oblivious was when Agata shrieked up the stairs "IT IS THE HOUR!"

With such a limited dream repertoire I was disposed of once and for all on the first morning.

"Stones," Agata read, having turned to the appropriate page in *I MIEI SOGNI*, in which almost every conceivable and inconceivable sort of animal, vegetable, mineral, man-made object and human being dream, except those thought by the author or publisher to be indecent, was listed in alphabetical order and its significance explained. "To see stones on the ground means that your way will be hard and difficult."

"You didn't throw stones, did you?" she said.

"No, I was just picking them up and dropping them."

"That's a good thing," she said severely, as if I had any control over what I dreamt, "if you had been throwing stones it would mean that you are going to behave badly towards a certain person."

– Eric Newby

---

the need for more restraint in your life and a longing for a more secure – even restricted – existence. If you feel fear or repression in this environment, this symbol may stand for another 'institution' which you feel is enforcing an alien or stringent code of behaviour on you.

Money Money is quite often a symbol for power, and the ability to change your life or conditions. If you dream that you're suddenly inundated with money, this could be a strong sign of dissatisfaction with some aspect of your life and the wish to change it radically. To be surrounded by money in any number of forms could indicate your feeling that the answer to your problems is available if you could only find it. If you find yourself wasting or destroying money in your dream or – on closer examination – find that the money is counterfeit or 'play' money, this could indicate a questioning of conventional values with which you are being presented.

Moon A strong symbol of both unattainability and beauty. The moon quite often represents someone to whom you feel strongly drawn yet who you feel is beyond your reach.

Mountains Clear symbols of challenge, hardship and accomplishment, mountains in your dream could represent some element in your life which you feel you must conquer. The proximity of the mountains could indicate just how you see yourself in relation to this challenge. If you find yourself standing on the summit yet still feel unsatisfied, this could indicate that you doubt the real value of what you are trying to do.

Mud A symbol of both impurity and of some element which you fear could keep you from some desired accomplishment. To find yourself sinking in mud or other sticky substance could indicate a fear of illness or death.

Museum This is a metaphor for order, classification and inactivity which could indicate that you doubt the vitality of some activity or situation in which you are involved. If, suddenly, in the midst of the museum something unusual or atypical takes place, this could be your own unconscious desire for change and a break of routine.

Music This is a strong symbol for elements of your past with which you associate a particular song or piece of music. If you recall a familiar tune, this may be your link with a particular time or setting or person in your life with which you connect the music in question. If you dream of strange, unfamiliar or discordant music, this may indicate that you feel threatened by a lack of familiar order in some aspect of your life.

Myths To find yourself dreaming of mythological settings, beings or beasts could indicate a desire for more elements of creativity or irrationality in your life. You may feel hemmed in by the ordinariness of your life and long for some excitement and colour.

A Very Bonnie Dream

I dream of everyone in the whole world being healthy and happy like one big family. No loneliness or poverty or fighting; then everyone could enjoy their lives to the full as we were meant to!

— Bonnie Langford

N

Nails A classic image of real or imagined persecution, the image of nails in a threatening context can indicate that you feel threatened – unjustly – by forces or people which do not understand you or your motivation.

Nakedness This is a symbol of utmost vulnerability, and if you find yourself naked – or semi-naked – in your dream, this may indicate that in some aspect of your life you feel exposed and at risk, especially in an emotional sense. But your own attitude towards your nakedness may tell you more about its meaning in your dream than the nakedness itself. If you are terribly embarrassed or worried about it and seek to cover yourself, this could indicate that you feel you have something to hide from the eyes – and understanding – of the world. If, on the other hand, you seem completely unconcerned at being naked, this may indicate a desire on your part to be seen as you really are, not as appearances, position, titles or possessions make you seem. If others in your dream are naked, this may indicate your need to feel superior, to have an advantage over the people around you.

Neighbours This is very often a symbol of people who, though not literally neighbours, are closest to you in some – not always positive – way. This 'closeness' can take the form of real or imagined pressure which you feel is being exerted on you in some role in your life. If, for instance, you dream that your boss or co-worker occupies the house next to yours, it may mean that you feel under pressure at work. On the other hand, if someone you like or want to know better appears in your dream as a close neighbour, this could indicate a desire to get closer to that person.

Night If your dream seems to turn day into night so that usual daytime activities now take place under artificial light, this could indicate that you feel that some aspect of your everyday life is unreal or pointless and a waste of 'valuable' or 'fruitful' time during the day. On the other hand, if the night of your dream is really dark, unlit by ordinary light sources, this could reflect your desire to keep some activity 'in the dark'.

Nightmares There is a theory that a nightmare is only the magnified extension of a waking fear,

A Taxi Just In Time

I am what is known as a lucid dreamer. That is, I can actually control my dreams while I'm having them. If I find myself, for example, dreaming that I'm stuck in heavy traffic and can't get a taxi to get to the station to catch a train to do some work (a classic dream for an overworked person like me), I can actually say to myself in my dream, 'this is only a dream — and it is my dream. Therefore I can do what I like with it, and I want a taxi, and a taxi is now going to come round the corner in this dream with its light on and whisk me to where I want to go'. And so it does.

I think lucid dreaming and novel-writing are very linked; in some ways, when you're writing a story — and certainly when *I'm* writing a story — the experience is somewhat dreamlike in that the characters take over and the events run themselves. I find myself sitting at my typewriter chronicling what's happening rather than inventing it in any conscious way. So dreams can be very useful to some of us.

— Claire Rayner

tension or problem into the realm of dreams where the very lack of reality and ordinary boundaries enbles it to grow out of all proportion. It can be futile to try to analyse the particular features of nightmares as they may bear no literal resemblance to their real-life counterparts. It may help, however, if you try to ignore the specifically frightening elements of nightmares and concentrate on the underlying roots of the images which terrify you. By taking the images out of an emotional context, you may be able to neutralise them or put them into a more realistic proportion. If you *know* you are having a nightmare and thus can detach yourself from its immediacy, this may symbolise your ability to stand back from emotional dilemmas.

Nudity (as opposed to nakedness) The distinction is lost on some people, but if in your dream others accept, or you are somehow convinced, that you are nude and not *naked*, this may indicate your desire to neutralise and put at a remove some threatening element or other in your waking life. If you dream that you are a nude model before a class of artists, this could indicate that you feel you are not showing off your talents or abilities as well as you could be.

The night before the Roman Emperor Caligula (12–47 AD) was assassinated, he dreamed that he was standing beside Jupiter's heavenly throne, when the God kicked him with the great toe of his right foot and sent him tumbling down to earth.

– from The Twelve Caesars, by Seutonius (c. 120 AD)

Numbers The potency and universality of numbers as dream symbols is well known. The interpretation of the meaning of numbers which seem to dominate your dreams is difficult, but there are certain signposts which may guide you:

One: very likely this number refers directly or indirectly back to you, 'Number One', and its meaning divined by analysing any emotion directed towards this number.

Two: the symbol of pairing or attachment, this number could indicate a strong desire to form a permanent bond with another.

Three: the symbolic number of opposition and jealousy. The triangle with its opposed sides and the love 'triangle' both have powerful connotations of tension and negative emotions.

Four: a symbol of order, sequence and completion of natural cycles and events such as the four seasons, the basic elements of earth, fire, water and wind, and the four equal sides of the strongest geometric shape, the square. This is a comforting number which suggests stability and contentment.

Five: the number of normality and humanity symbolising the five fingers and five toes of the human being.

Six: can be a sinister number with heavy connotations of black magic (666 – the Sign of the Beast) and other disturbing deviations from the normal and orthodox.

Seven: the number symbolic of luck, contentedness and good fortune suggesting that fortune is definitely on your mind.

Eight: the number of infinity and continuity which suggests a completeness or wholeness to some endeavour.

Nine: an ambiguous, negative ('nein' – 'no') number which suggests a state of transition or incompletion.

Zero: a number suggesting perfectibility and perfection. It reflects the wholeness of life and yet also symbolises nothingness and the egg which is the beginning of life.

Some specific combinations of numbers in your dream can be interpreted together:

10 or 100: perfection, the best a thing can be.

69: obvious sexual connotations suggesting a fear of taboo and unorthodoxy.

88: an even stronger image of continuity or the infinity of possibilities.

212: (or 100 depending on context): could suggest heat or a feeling of pressure.

666: strongly suggestive of evil and the occult; a warning.

Numbness A pervasive sense of numbness or lack of emotion in your dream, a feeling of being 'packed in cotton wool', could indicate that you are deliberately stifling emotions in an effort to protect yourself from some emotional danger.

No Way Out

I wouldn't say that I dream at all these days, though I'm told we all do so I suppose I just don't remember my dreams.

But, for a period of two or three years, when my children were young and before I became an 'agony aunt', I used to have a recurring dream which unhappily I could always recall only too well: I was in a small room with a single exit. It was empty except for me and one of those old-fashioned, round cushiony seats which were called 'dumpties' or 'pouffes'. I would start to walk out of the room but, when I did, this crazy object would flip to its side and roll towards the door, getting bigger and bigger until it blocked the doorway and I couldn't get out.

In the dream, I never escaped from that room. But the dreams stopped so, in a way, I did.

— *Angela Willans*

'I had a dream last night. An amputated head had been stuck onto a man's trunk, making him look like a drunken actor. The head began to talk. I was terrifed and knocked over my folding screen in trying to push a Russian in front of me against the furious creature's onslaught.'

— *August Strindberg (1849–1912), Swedish dramatist*

O

Oasis A cliché symbol of physical salvation, a desirable – but perhaps illusory – promise which can be the dreamer's way of expressing longing for some hoped-for reward or answer to some deep desire. If you actually get to the oasis and it is false or dry or disappointing, this could be your dream warning you against false expectations.

Oaths If your dream features a solemn oath or vow, this could reflect your unconscious feeling that you are not fulfilling some obligation or responsibility in your life.

Obligations The feeling, in a dream, that you *must* do something or be something can be an echo of your knowledge that someone is counting strongly on you.

Obscene The strong and repellent imagery of something obscene or forbidden in your dream could be a reaction to a struggle within yourself to do 'the decent thing' in some real-life situation.

Obstacles If your dream keeps throwing up obstacles or barriers to your progress, it could be a sign that you are ambivalent about the achievement of some specific personal or career goal. It's almost as if your dream is telling you: *Be careful what you ask for; you may get it.*

Off limits A dream landscape which includes some area which is clearly forbidden or out of bounds to the dreamer may indicate some area of his unconscious mind which he feels it would be dangerous to enter. Determining just what area this is is difficult, but your dream may include certain clues or directions.

Oil This is one of those double-edged symbols for both harmony and peacefulness and – in a more modern sense – pollution and the discordance and noise of machinery. Which – if either of these – it is in your dreams will depend on the context of the oil or substitute and how you seem to feel about it.

Old people A preponderance of aged figures in your dream could indicate that you feel that you are wasting you life, that in a sense they represent yourself in terms of lost opportunities and frustration.

Olympic symbol (or athletic contests. This symbol which has permeated our consciousness could suggest that you feel involved in some struggle – likely nothing to do with the physical or athletic – which could raise you above the crowd if you are successful.

Omnipotence This feeling, especially if it pervades every aspect of your dream, can indicate that you feel weak and helpless in your everyday life.

Onion A common symbol for a mystery which your unconscious mind feels needs unravelling to get at the core of some situation or other.

Opera Whether or not you can sing, if you dream that you are at – or in – an opera or other lavish and overcharged performance, this could indicate that you feel some aspect of your life is being overdramatised or blown up out of realistic proportion.

Opposition If in your dream you feel that everything – other people, the elements, the very geography or landscape – are opposed to you, this could indicate that you feel a need for constructive opposition in some aspect of your life and feel danger in too much freedom.

Oxygen This is a potent symbol of life itself, usually invisible and taken absolutely for granted. If you become conscious of this element in your dream, it could mean that you feel aware of your dependence on the basics of life for your survival. This could be a reminder and an expression of your vulnerability in some situation.

P

Packing A major metaphor for anticipation or preparation for change, to dream that you are packing may indicate that your unconscious is telling you that you are ready for some important transition in your life. If you can remember exactly what you were packing, how appropriate the items seemed at the time, the ease or difficulty of the task, whether anyone attempted to stop you,

who else was there, it may help you to understand more about the import of this symbol.

Paralysis An image suggesting indecision or inner conflict. To be unable – wholly or partially – to move in your dream could indicate that in some important respect you feel an emotional 'paralysis' which stops you from doing something you know you

I dreamed that Max, Otto and I had the habit of packing our trunks only when we reached the railway station. There we were, carrying our shirts, for example, through the main hall to our distant trunks. Although this seemed to be a general custom, it was not a good one in our case, especially since we had begun to pack only shortly before the arrival of the train. Then we were naturally excited and had hardly any hope of still catching the train, let alone getting good seats.

– Franz Kafka (1883–1924), Czech writer,
his diary entry for 28 October 1911

should do. This could be considered a 'wishful' dream in that you could be trying to avoid something which seems inevitable.

Passport A requirement for 'important' travel or changes. To dream about having this document could mean that you feel you are ready for change. On the other hand, if you have lost or can't find your passport – or it is mutilated or destroyed or belonging to someone else – this could indicate that you are looking for excuses not to make some move or decision.

Photograph Many experts have considered this to be the symbol of the soul or the real 'self' of the dreamer. Sometimes the image is idealised; at other times the dreamer is shocked to be portrayed as aged, ill or in some unhappy circumstance. Generally, this is an image which may be considered a form of 'search', a re-evaluation of life position and goals. Careful attention to the detail and setting of the photograph may tell you much about your attitude and reaction to this self-inventory.

Plants A metaphor for health and well-being, plants in your dream can give you a clue to your own feelings about how your life is going.

Poison A powerful image suggesting potential for death and destruction. This may not be a literal reference – and it probably isn't – but the presence of, or even the taking of, poison in your dream could indicate the 'death' of some aspiration or ambition or even a strong urge to make a transition into 'another existence'. Also, poison could be a symbol of some other danger you feel threatens you.

Police A basic authority figure which could represent in your dream any person or institution which you feel has authority over your life. The actions of the police in your dream and your attitude towards them could indicate your own inner judgement of some aspect of your life. Your reaction to the police figures could also symbolise your own reactions to authority. If the policeman is – or becomes – someone you know, this could indicate that you feel under some control or observation from this source.

Portrait This could be a symbol of maturation and the inevitability that life always leads to death. Like a photograph, a portrait captures an instant in life which is forever gone, yet forever frozen, and your attitude towards the image represented in the portrait could tell you how you feel about your present state of life and how you feel your progress relates to some greater plan. A portrait can also represent the unchangeable nature of the past, and your attitude towards the image could tell you how you evaluate your accomplishments so far.

Prayer One of the greatest symbols of the sacrifice of volition. To dream that you are praying or that your prayers are answered could indicate that you feel able to surrender some degree of independence to an outside force or authority.

The Lazy Turtle

I am not a great dreamer, but I do have one recurring dream – many, many times. I am a turtle, swimming in an idyllic tropical sea; in the distance there is an island, with palm trees, and beside me are various seals, penguins(!) and dolphins playing around. I am doing nothing except float and laze.

What a psychiatrist will make of that one I just do not know!

My mother (who was a very clever artist) even painted the scene from my description...

– Patrick Moore

Pregnancy Though this *could* be a literal symbol, it is more likely to represent hope and expectation for some project or undertaking. A pregnancy which seems interminable or very exaggerated could indicate a feeling of impatience that something is not happening as fast as you think it should. In some circumstances, dream pregnancy can be taken as a symbol for punishment or guilt for some act of the dreamer. It is also a symbol of the unknown.

Prison A strong symbol for frustration, the prison of your dreams could be a representation of how you perceive some aspect of your life. Careful analysis of the circumstances of your 'imprisonment' can provide clues as to what element you feel has you in this situation. Very important are the other figures – if any – in prison. If you are all alone, this could indicate that the metaphorical prison is loneliness and isolation. Try to remember the figures – if any – who were keeping you imprisoned. If in your dream you were near – but not in – prison, this could indicate that you feel that some restriction on your life and choices threatens you.

Punishment No matter who is doing the punishing in your dream, this is almost always self-inflicted. But there is no reason to assume that you need to be punished or even *want* to punish yourself. The subconscious can present a very subtle version of reality through your dreams. If you dream repeatedly about punishment, you might consider carefully whether you are being too harsh or judgemental about yourself or some of your actions.

Q

Quack This is a universally reviled and ridiculed figure – whether medical or of some other profession – and generally can be taken as a symbol for dissatisfaction, usually in yourself, and expresses the feeling that you are cheating or not making the maximum effort at some task.

Quadruplets (or other multiple births) Very seldom a literal symbol, more likely to sign that your energies or attentions are divided among a number of directions or goals. A symbol of confusion.

Qualifications To dream that you are working towards or are being awarded some qualification that you lack could be an expression of the feeling that you are somehow inferior in that you lack some theoretical quality considered necessary. If the qualification seems nonsensical or irrelevant, this could reflect your attitude towards your job or other endeavour.

Quarrelling This phenomenon in a dream is usually the dreamer quarrelling with himself or attempting to weigh in his unconscious some important decision or dilemma. If the quarrel is seemingly resolved in your dream, this may indicate that your unconscious has come to a decision, though it may not be obvious in your waking life.

Quarry To dream that you are the quarry of some kind of a hunt or search may indicate that you feel under pressure in some aspect of your life and seek to hide away.

Quarry (rock or other) A symbol which strongly suggests that you feel you have inner resources and abilities which would be revealed if only someone cared enough to search for them.

Quay (wharf, dock) A comforting symbol of security, homecoming, and an end to danger and exposure (or conversely, the beginning of these), but a clear sign of transition from one state or role to another.

Queen Generally speaking this dream creature is a clear reflection of your mother or other strong maternal figure. As with other personifications, the actions of this figure and your attitude towards her may combine to shed light on the relationship.

Quest A symbol for your desire to investigate some aspect of your life and relationships with the aim of finding some goal which may not be clear to your conscious mind.

Question If a particular question or set of questions – however simple – is repeated over and over in your dream, this may well be an indication that there is some nagging matter preying on your unconscious mind which wants answering.

Quiet A deathly silence in your dream, perhaps despite the presence of people, objects and other elements which one would expect to make noise, can mean that you feel besieged by sound – and perhaps problems – in your life and are seeking escape from them in your dream world.

Quilt Usually made of bright and multicoloured scraps of cloth, this image could suggest that you are very aware of all the different life roles you are playing and that you are striving to bring all of the different elements of your life into harmony.

Quitting If you find yourself quitting a job – or other position, function or role – in your dreams, this very likely could be an indication that you feel under-appreciated and seek more obvious approval from family, peers and superiors.

Quixotic (or heroic) The adoption of this role in your dream might suggest that you seek attention in ways which do not present themselves in everyday life. A careful study of the beneficiaries of your heroism might reveal unexpected attitudes of which you are not consciously aware.

A Novel Source

I had a dream about a chaotic hotel, where all the reservations had got muddled up; the dead and the living kept arriving in the same taxis. It was as if everyone was on a group-honeymoon. But not everything was pleasant; a snake, a bushmaster, was discovered coiled behind a deepfreeze.

Whatever it meant – and I believe it's a protest against death and separation – it proved a potent image, for a poem came out of it and, a year or so later, the chaotic hotel turned into a novel, *The White Hotel*. The power of the unconscious, to which we must listen!

– *D.M. Thomas*

A Battle

Laying on my bed that night,
Just fallen asleep,
The visions inside my head,
Seemed to swallow me.

Down, down,
Into the land of dreams,
I went, did I,
Would I never stop?

I landed on a soft carpet,
Of soft and rich, smooth fur,
I saw a lady wearing Pink Satin,
She saw me before I saw her.

'Come here,' she said, 'Come here.'
In a voice as soft as silk,
I had to go to her,
Her voice was calling me.

'Hello,' said I,
'Hello,' she said,
'I have waited for you,
for three years and a day.'

'You must save us from the army,
You must save us from our king.'

'But how?' asked I,
'But where and when and why?'

'You must stop our war,' said she.
'You complete our army.'
So I got on a horse,
and rode out and away.

We got to the battle,
Just as it began
Someone knocked her off her horse
And I heard her cry.

One moment she was there,
The next she was not,
Did she have an invisible cloak?
Or did she not?

Her voice echoed round my room,
Then just in my head,
Was she there?
Was she dead?

I was no longer in the land of dreams,
So I shall never know,
What happened to that lady,
In my dream so long ago.

Rosanna Farthorne
Shiplake C.E. School
Age 10

R

Rabbi Like a priest or other clerical figure, a rabbi could represent forces in life which the dreamer feels are – or could – sit in judgement on some behaviour which might be less than honourable, or even illegal. If the dreamer is not Jewish, or possibly not even religious, the dream rabbi could express the dreamer's *need* to be judged or hemmed in by a force of moral law.

Rabies A dog or other animal with – or suspected of having – rabies could represent some person or thing which your unconscious considers dangerous to your emotional well-being. The dream setting in which this image appears may well indicate who or what it symbolises.

Racing This a true symbol of competition, though the competition may not be – and probably is not – physical. If it is a two-person race, this could indicate the dreamer's effort to choose from equally attractive or repellent alternatives. If the race is grossly unfair or imbalanced, this could be the dreamer's subconscious questioning the justice of some competition.

Rack This antiquated and outmoded instrument of torture still serves as a dream symbol for coercion and force applied in order to command answers to questions which the dreamer may not even recognise. The person on the rack – whatever form taken – almost always represents the dreamer. If there is no-one on the rack, this dream could represent a self-warning of a trying situation ahead.

Radio In some instances, this can represent an electronic version of your conscience in that it is a voice seemingly coming from nowhere. If what is heard on the radio seems to have some bearing on a current situation or dilemma in your life, it may be your unconscious speaking.

Raffle A symbol of chance and opportunity, though if the prize offered or won is either insignificant or downright repulsive, this could represent the danger in aspiring to gain something without carefully weighing the consequences.

Rage This emotion may seem undirected or directed at some seemingly innocuous entity, but it could be the dreamer's unconscious disappointment with himself for some failure known only to him.

Rain A common expression of the need of all living organisms for the elements without which life cannot be maintained. In many cases, this rain will represent not literal necessities but some metaphorical quality or value which the dreamer feels that his life is lacking. Figuratively, the rain could be spiritual renewal and invigoration.

The Senoi indians of Malaysia are taught from infancy to face and overcome dream monsters, to embrace pleasant dream experiences and to go on exploratory flights to unknown places.

Raisins (other dried fruit) These can be taken as a symbol for the passing of time and the literal physical drying out as the human being ages. This image could indicate that you are aware of time passing and the need to make the most of it.

Rape Among the most violent of dream images, this could symbolise not the physical act but the unconscious fear of symbolic and intellectual degradation from some source. Rape is also a powerful and evocative metaphor for helplessness and the domination by the strong – physical, mental or emotional – over the weak. If the dreamer seems to be the rapist, this could be imagery calling into question the morality of some intellectual act.

Rats Powerful images reflecting self-disgust and fear of danger from some dark recess of the mind. A classic ingredient of nightmares, but very rarely a literal translation in dream imagery of some waking fear. Far more likely an intellectual metaphor.

Reaction The dreamer's feeling of strong reaction to some element of a dream may indicate that the unconscious mind is trying to wrestle with and dissipate strong emotional feelings which the dreamer has buried in some social or public situation.

Rebel This colourful symbol, reinforced by images from films or other stock images for rebellion against authority, may indicate the dreamer's desire – perhaps long suppressed – to achieve a personal revolt against some influence or force which the dreamer feels is repressive.

Recklessness The feeling of being perfectly unconcerned with any possibility of danger – perhaps despite vivid dream representations of menace – could symbolise your feeling that life is too dull and stultified and in need of the colour of some excitement.

Referee (umpire, or other) A strong symbol of justice and order which could indicate that the dreamer feels in a situation in which the external application of a strong code of behaviour is required.

Regimentation If the dreamer feels that some force, whether in his dream or exerted from outside, is somehow commanding him – and most likely others – blindly to follow a set of rules or procedures, this could be a direct reflection of the dreamer's attitude towards some authority or strong figure in his waking life.

Rescue Either dramatic or more prosaic, the phenomenon of being rescued – or rescuing another – can refer to some deeply felt but less dramatic representation of a human relationship which the dreamer feels is in need of strengthening.

Reunion (or other emotional gathering) This powerfully nostalgic image can symbolise the dreamer's strong need for some form of belonging or membership quite at odds with a waking behaviour which may stress independence and rationality rather than emotion.

Riding A powerful image of domination and the exercise of the will of one over another, the seeming relationship between horse and rider (usually the

dreamer) can have a close approximation to the true attitude of the dreamer to some person or authority in waking life. This pairing can also represent the ambivalence of the relationship involving domination and changes which can take place in such a relationship.

Ring (wedding, engagement or denoting membership of an organisation) This symbol usually represents loyalty and fidelity to some person or institution, and the dreamer's attitude towards the ring may indicate true feelings towards the same in waking life.

Ropes These are images which can take on a multitude of meanings depending on the context and role in which they appear. This can range from ties which hold the dreamer back to a lifeline which saves the dreamer from danger. Ropes can also represent a strong skein of relationships on which the dreamer depends and from which he rebels.

Royalty (or other beings exalted by their dress or reception by others) These figures of respect and veneration usually symbolise the dreamer's parents or other intimate personifications of authority.

'The gods sent not our dreams, we make our own.'

– Robert Burton (1577–1640), English clergyman and author

S

Sacrifices Whether this is a literal sacrifice or a metaphorical one, it usually suggests some area of your life where you feel that you are having to give up something which, if you had your choice, you would rather keep.

Salt A standard symbol for preservation, the presence of salt in your dream could suggest some element in your life which is at risk. Salt also suggests an enhancer of flavour in some other element or activity.

Scales (weighing) Strongly suggestive of some aspect of justice or judgement, the setting in which you see the scales and their condition can tell you a lot about the particular significance of this symbol to you.

School If you are an adult, this is a strong symbol of regression, of an unconscious urge to go back to childhood and avoid adult responsibility, especially if you experience particular happiness in your dream. On the other hand, school is the usual setting for learning and to dream of one could be an expression of a deep urge to learn.

Searching This common dream – the search which never seems to end and often has no conscious object – could be an expression of a deep-seated feeling in your waking life that something is lacking from your life.

Servants A symbol of affluence far outside of the realm of reality, the servants in your dream could

---

In Burma, it is a common belief that the soul is like a butterfly which leaves the body through the mouth and wanders to places where the dreamer has previously been.

---

represent your own qualities and abilities which – if properly used – could lift you out of the ordinary and into a life offering many more material goods.

Sex Though many of our dreams are dominated by sex and sexual urges, it is by no means certain that even explicit sexual images and acts can be so routinely interpreted. Probably more important than the literal representation of sexual aspects of your dreams is your own attitude – if you can divine it – towards sex in your dreams. Since sex is one of the most powerful and yet forbidden aspects of our lives, it is natural that it should be represented in our dreams in many different ways.

Shadowy figures Often featured in so-called nightmares, shadowy figures which are never fully revealed may represent elements of your life which are not fully developed, the potential of which you are aware but which is not yet manifest.

Shoes These are common images of travel or transition, and a dominance of shoe images in your dreams could indicate that your unconscious is preoccupied with the prospect of a change or move.

Shooting (a gun) A very common symbol of aggression in which your anger is taken beyond the realm of waking expression and heightened by this dramatic and exaggerated image. If you are trying to shoot, but the bullets are having no effect or the gun will not fire at all, this could represent some area of impotence or helplessness you feel. Even if you know your dream target, he or she may not be the true object of your aggressive feelings.

Shopkeeping This prosaic image may represent in your dreams an effort to add up or calculate your life in terms of achievements and failures – the totting up of a bill which must be paid.

My Dream

When I was eight I had a weird dream. It was Monday morning before school. I was getting my school books ready. I got to school and went to my class and started work. I was the best in my class. I got every single thing right. After school I went to the woods near my house to do my homework. There was a lady there with a painting. She looked a bit like Miss Hardbroom in 'The Worst Witch'. I sat down. I was just about to leave when the lady came over and gave me an apple. When I put it in my bag she lifted her hands and it was like she put a spell on me. The next day at school I was the worst in the class and I was sent to the headmaster. I thought the lady must have done it. So I had an idea. I went back to the wood the next day and the spell was released and I woke up.

– Julie Saunders
Shiplake Primary School

Exams, Exams

My recurrent nightmare is having to take Physics A-level again. Now it's evolving into having to take *any* exam again....

— *Jancis Robinson*

Skiing To dream that you are hurtling downhill on skis can indicate that you feel that some element of your life is out of order and possibly endangering you, though not necessarily in a literal sense.

Sleep This common symbol of escape can have its roots in a desire for simple evasion of some responsibility or a longing for the most profound sleep of all – death. To dream that you are sleeping and cannot be wakened may indicate that you fear the consequences of some act which could be delayed by not waking and having to face it.

Snow A symbol for purity which can also be confused or mixed up with the concept of emotional coldness and reserve. If you find the snow warm rather than cold, this could indicate that you find emotional safety in the coldness of reserve.

Soldier The essence of the soldier's life is discipline. To dream of being – or being surrounded by – soldiers could indicate a desire for more discipline in your life and with it a surrender of responsibility for important actions. Soldiers marching in formation can also be considered a symbol of harmony. A dead soldier could represent fear of commitment to an ideal which may require action and thus danger, even if it is not physical.

Spectacles Since spectacles almost always make us see better, the spectacles in your dream may be a symbol for insight made all the stronger because spectacles are put on and taken off, just as often we lack insight not because we can't see but because we will ourselves not to see clearly. Broken spectacles can be a symbol for some knowledge and understanding that is lost to you for reasons beyond your control. They could also indicate that you are refusing to see something very obvious in your life which could be painful.

Sphere A symbol of unity and wholeness, especially if connected with growing plants.

Stairs Very likely a symbol for ambition and advancement if going up, of declining vigour and fortune if going down. Endless stairs can suggest that you see no way out of a situation.

Stars A very strong symbol not only of success and aspiration beyond the usual but also of understanding and reason in the face of mystery and obscurity. If the stars seem to form some shape or answer you are seeking, this may mean that you seek the answer to a puzzle.

Statue A symbol both of exaltation and death in that statues are very seldom made to commemorate either the living or the humble. A statue of yourself in your dream could indicate that you feel undervalued and that you deserve better.

Storms Almost always an emotional metaphor which suggests that you are failing in your waking hours to express deeply held emotions, possibly of a violent sort. Dreams may be an outlet for 'stormy' feelings you repress in your family, working or social life.

Stranger This familiar dream figure, the stranger who either never fully emerges or who seems to know you very well though not known to you, may represent your strong urge to understand more about your own nature and capabilities.

Success A symbol of frustration and wishful thinking. Often dream success can be a substitute for a lack of that same quality in your life. Success in your dreams which seems empty can be a warning against false values and rewards.

Sun A metaphor for power, energy and light, the sun symbolises the life force and a phenomenon without which human life would not be possible. This can be a strongly religious image which transcends parochialism and may indicate a desire to get at ultimate truth and meaning.

Surgery This can figuratively symbolise your desire to probe beneath the surface and get at some truth or reality which seems to elude your efforts to uncover it. If *you* are the surgeon, this could indicate that you feel that you have the power to resolve some important matter.

Swastika A strong symbol of evil and domination which suggests that you fear danger from some source which you consider ruthless.

T

Talking A dream which features an inordinate amount of talking could indicate that the dreamer feels the need to express closely held feelings that in waking life are perhaps kept within.

Task If a dream seems to be dominated by a single overwhelming task or goal, this could be the dreamer's unconscious telling him that something of emotional importance is left undone in his life and that he'll receive no rest until it is done.

Teachers Such authority figures are very often overlapped by or merged with symbols of the dreamer's father and often it is difficult to get through the various guises the father figure wears. If a teacher clearly turns into your father or vice versa, this could indicate that something in your life goes against or would not live up to the standards your father set.

Teeth (losing them) This is a definite metaphor for maturing and therefore for aging. If the dreamer's teeth fall out or feel loose in his gums, this could be a premonition of the ravages of old age and ultimately death and a reminder that life is short.

Telephone If your dream finds you talking on the telephone to a particular person – especially one you see every day – this could indicate that you feel a barrier or reserve between you and that person. If the phone rings persistently but there is nobody on it when you answer it, this could suggest that you feel that you are missing out on some vital information necessary to your life.

Thirst (see hunger)

Thunderstorm This powerful natural force could be a religious symbol reminding the dreamer of the god-like power of nature and the relative insignificance of man in the face ot it. The boom of the thunder could be allied with the commanding voice of a superior force telling you what to do.

Time Perhaps the most plastic element in your dream, time is such a variable that it is usually relevant only as it connects with other elements in dreams, such as setting, light, emotions and colour. But a pervasive sense that time is passing fast or that time is a finite rather than infinite resource could be your unconscious telling you that you are wasting valuable opportunities in your life.

Tools Various labouring or craft tools in your dreams are likely not to be taken literally but may be symbols of some hidden capacity or goal of which you may not even be aware.

Tower An obvious sexual symbol, this image can also be taken as a representative for some lofty goal or authority which retains an important position in your life.

Toys These are very common symbols of either your real childhood or the child-like essence and nature of man. If the toys suddenly become unpleasant or dangerous, this could be a symbol of the pitfall of looking backwards towards an allegedly happy time of innocence rather than looking forward to maturity.

Transformation This intriguing but not uncommon phenomenon of a figure in your dream transforming itself into yet another familiar entity offers you the opportunity to ponder the connections between seemingly opposite concepts or images.

Treasure Whatever form this takes, it is very likely to be the realisation of that which you value most in your life. Your attitude towards the 'treasure' is a definite indication that your attention is being focused on some important element in your life.

Tree This is a potent symbol of the deep-rootedness of the life force and, in the more figurative sense, of regeneration and the

---

A Royal Command

I was sitting at home watching Going Live when I had a phone call from the Queen asking if I could go to Buckingham Palace for tea. So I went there and in the lounge sitting at a table was the Queen and the head of Police. As I sat down the Queen said that I would make a great head-of-Police as I was so young and no one would know it was me. I said yes. So I was taken to my new office. My first job was to go to a football match and mingle with the crowds. Suddenly a fan pushes forward and I wake up. I hope that I was a hero.

Ian Hough
Shiplake School
Age 11

To Sleep...Perchance to Dream

How often have I wished I could drift into a dreamy wonderland. Instead, the moment my head hits the pillow, I rarely remember a thing until dawn. It must be the sleep of the exhausted, not the just, because if I was due to face the electric chair the next morning, I'm sure I'd still sleep like the traditional log!

The rare night that I do dream, you can bet your boots that I'll wake at a cliff hanger, and never manage to recapture the plot – (perhaps hold back on that cheese board when I shouldn't). Even the odd nightmare is so rare that it leaves me panting for more.

It's a pity I'll never be able to swop dreams, or claim even one premonition that came true, but, being the positive creature I am, I shall count my blessings that I never wake up in a muck sweat of fear, and will be quite happy to say to others, 'Goodnight – sweet dreams!'

– Katie Boyle

cycles of nature in that trees tend to 'die' in winter yet are resurrected in the spring. If the trees in your dream are dead, dying or unhealthy, this could be a telling indication of your unconscious vitality.

Triangle This is a basic symbol for balance, especially of the various elements of your life. If the triangle seems out of balance, misshapen or incomplete, you may be worried that a particular element of your life is asserting too much influence or dominance over others.

Tunnel This is a symbol of transition from one state to another, specifically the most basic transition of all – birth – but your dream passage through a tunnel can represent almost any major movement or change in your life. As with many basic symbols, your attitude towards the tunnel and going through it are very important clues.

Twins A symbol of duality, specifically the two sides of your own personality or nature. Often these images – though identical – manifest great disparities in emotional content or impact.

U

U-boat A strong symbol of menace representing some element in your life or environment – probably much less dramatic – which is presently out of sight but which may 'attack' suddenly and without warning.

Ugliness If it seems to you that most elements in your dream are ugly and repugnant to you, this may indicate a tendency to find unpleasantness in aspects of life which most people would find acceptable and thus represents a negative period of your life which is coming out in your dreams.

Ulcer (or other sharp or persistent pain deep within) This could be a strong indication that some aspect of your life – some personal situation or relationship – is niggling away at you in the way that an ulcer does the human body.

Ultimatum If something in your dream seems to be giving you a final warning, this may be an indication that your unconscious is telling you that some condition in your waking life must be changed for peace of mind.

Umbilical cord An obvious symbol of attachment and dependence. This – either literally or figuratively portrayed – could represent some bond which you know must eventually be broken. If the cord is impossible to sever or seems to grow together again, this is an indication that you are finding some dependent relationship especially difficult to end.

Umbrella A common security and defence symbol which could indicate that you feel in need of a psychological 'umbrella' to shield you from something that you find emotionally threatening.

Umpire A common authority figure which could symbolise either your need for a judgemental figure in your life or your own conscience which is judging you.

Unbalanced If elements in your dream seem out of perspective or balance, this could suggest your unconscious need for balance in life and your feeling of unease at a lack of control concerning some element of your life.

Uncivilised A barbaric or primitive being in your dream could be the representation of this aspect of your life or personality which gives vent to the unacceptable part of your makeup kept under wraps in 'normal' life.

Under-exposed If your dreams seem faint and vague like an under-exposed photograph, this could indicate that you feel that some element in your life needs further development to give satisfaction.

Underground If your dream seems to be taking place underground or in a cavern of some sort, this could symbolise your feeling that some activity in which you are involved needs to be kept from examination.

Uniforms If your dream is populated by people wearing uniforms – recognisable or not – this could suggest that you feel your life is too constricted by authority. If *you* are in uniform, it could be that you feel anonymous and without individual responsibility in your role in life, like a soldier in an army.

Unmasked A character in your dream which removes a mask or is unmasked by some other means could represent someone in your life who you feel is keeping real feelings from you.

Uproar Noise and confusion in your dream could represent your feeling that some element of your life is more disordered than it seems to the outside world.

I dreamed that somebody was dead. I don't know who, but it's not to the purpose. It was a private gentleman, and a particular friend; and I was greatly overcome when the news was broken to me (very delicately) by a gentleman in a cocked hat, top boots, and a sheet. Nothing else. 'Good God,' I said, 'is he dead?'

'He is dead, sir,' rejoined the gentleman, 'as a door-nail. But we all must die, Mr Dickens, sooner or later, my dear sir.'

'Ah,' I said, 'Yes to be sure. Very true. But what did he die of?' The gentleman burst into tears and said in a voice broken by emotion:

'He christened his youngest child, sir, with a toasting fork.'

I never in my life was so affected as at his having fallen a victim to this complaint. It carried a conviction to my mind that he never could have recovered. I knew that it was the most interesting and fatal malady in the world; and I wrung the gentleman's hand in a convulsion of respectful admiration, for I felt that this explanation did equal honour to his head and heart.

– Charles Dickens (1812–70), from a letter written on 1 September 1843

V

Vacant If some building – a house or office – which you expect to be occupied turns out to be devoid of population, this could suggest that this vacancy is a metaphor for some spiritual emptiness in an aspect of your life.

Vagabond A symbol of freedom and lack of responsibility which could indicate that you feel restrained in your life by ties of which you would like to be free. If the vagabond or tramp is unhappy or menacing, this could indicate the negative side of such freedom.

Valentine A symbol both of love and open communication of affection which could represent your desire to open up your feelings to someone who has no idea of your real feelings.

Valley A comforting symbol of protection and security from the elements and the richness which can come of a sheltering environment. If you seem unhappy in this atmosphere, it could mean that you feel overprotected.

Vampire A classic – even cliché – symbol for a life-draining force. The vampire in your dream could be any person or thing which you feel deprives you of necessary strength.

Vandalism If you or others in your dream destroy without reason this could indicate that in your waking life you are stifling negative instincts in an effort to seem more respectable than you really feel.

Vanishing If some person or thing in your dream suddenly vanishes without reason, this could suggest that you feel insecure in relation to someone or something in your waking life which you fear could do the same.

Vegetables A metaphor for less than human capabilities and understanding, a predominance of vegetables in your dream could indicate that you feel surrounded by those incapable of understanding the more sophisticated side of your makeup.

Vehicles (see journey)

Veil A woman wearing a veil in your dream could represent someone whom you think you know but who your unconscious tells you is keeping some facts or truths hidden from you. If the veil is lifted only to reveal yet another veil, this could express the futility of ever knowing all that you should know about another person.

Velvet A symbol of luxury, velvet and similar fabrics could be a symbol of your unconscious need to pamper yourself in an environment which you feel is stark and inhospitable.

Victory A victorious feeling in your dream – especially if it is unexplained or undeserved – could represent your feeling that you have accomplished a similar success in your waking life but one which is not generally recognised.

Vines These represent a strong symbol of entanglement and could suggest that there are elements in your life which you feel stifle your freedom or ability to move without hindrance.

Voice A voice in your dream which seems to come from nowhere – or everywhere – could indicate your need for guidance in some respect of your life.

Volcano A symbol suggesting an innocent object which conceals a destructive capability which could strike without warning.

Apple Dream

I have a friend called Jo who always wants bites of other people's apples; this dream's about her. In my dream I was eating an apple at break. I had taken one bite when Jo asked for a bite. I gave her the apple and she ate it in one bite. So I got another apple out of my pocket and took a bite. Again Jo ate it again and again. She had eaten six apples when I started pulling out oranges. After six oranges it was bananas; then I felt in my pocket and I found another apple. This time I just gave it to her. Then my other friend said, 'Megan, I slipped that into your pocket, it's a bomb!' Suddenly Jo took off and went wizzing up through the air then she came down and hit the ground, bong-g-g and I woke up.

Megan Hill
Shiplake School
age 10

Una Gets Left Behind

One of the most vivid and disconcerting dreams I have always remembered, was after the birth of my third son, and I dreamt myself, my husband and three sons were floating up to heaven – except they were miles ahead of me and they wouldn't slow down; they just kept looking down laughing at my weak efforts to keep up with them, nor would they listen to me calling to them. I was relieved to awaken, but I have only ever remembered that dream years later.

– Una Stubbs

W

Walls As obvious symbols of barriers, whether physical, emotional or intellectual, walls in your dream very likely represent those aspects of your life which you find most challenging. The wall which appears and disappears randomly can symbolise barriers which your unconscious tells you are illusory or of your own making. The wall which grows as you climb it or try to go around it could represent a barrier about which you can do nothing. A wall which contains a locked gate suggests that the key to the barrier is within your reach.

War A common metaphor for internal conflict, especially when the foes are identical or similar. The war in your dream could well represent a battle within yourself between conflicting goals or desires.

Water In all of its multifarious forms, water is a potent and significant dream symbol. In general, it is considered a representation of spiritual rebirth, the essence of the life force and a cleansing agent for the spirit. Because water takes so many forms, it offers a wide variety of contexts for interpretations:

Bathing: the purification of the human spirit.

Cloudy water: the human spirit and consciousness with all of its potential for power.

Dams: repression of vital instincts in an effort to control or channel them.

Deep water: the human unconscious.

Drought: an insufficiency of the life force or energy and consequent withering.

Flooding: the destructive

Panic Stations

The only recurring dream I have is of catching trains. I'm never catching it myself but I'm always in charge of someone in the family for whom it is vital they should be on that train and no other. The agony of getting them to the station is awful – I'm hurrying them through crowds and quite demented with the strain but they don't seem to care or even to know it *is* vital. Finding the platform, finding a seat, settling them in – it's all a battle and then the whistle goes (yes, I know we don't have whistles any more). I only just get off in time and collapse – and wake up. I once read dreams of trains mean death. Jolly lucky I always get off in time, then. And curiously enough, the people I put on these trains are always already dead – and seem happy.

– Margaret Forster

capacity inherent in basically lifegiving forces.

Flowing water: life's usual pace with its placidity and capacity for comfort.

Lagoons: hidden depths with inherent menace and danger.

Pools (artificial): man's efforts to capture and retain the spirit of nature.

Reflections in water: man's intrinsic search for meaning in his life and self, often with narcissistic overtones.

Rivers: the force of destiny which carries the dreamer to his ultimate goal.

The sea: the mystery and power inherent in nature, the ultimate source of all power in life.

Springs: the mysterious source of the wellspring of human life and an energising force.

Wells: the domestication of nature for the benefit of humanity and a captive source of life.

Weapons Symbols of aggression which give the dreamer a potent and dramatic vehicle, not always to be taken literally, for his feelings. The type of weapon may have significance, but the emotion of the dreamer in relation to it is likely to be more vital.

Wedding Not always what it signifies literally, the dream wedding can have connotations of any forthcoming alliance, however unromantic and prosaic. The others present at the wedding besides the two principals can give a powerful indication of the context in which it is taking place.

Wheel A symbol of both movement and chance with risk

as the principal common element.

Wind As one of the four elemental forces, the wind can be taken as a force which directs our destinies, both in its violence and its gentleness. You should especially note where the wind is directing you if this is discernible.

Window A symbol for the dreamer's outlook on life. Both what is seen from the window and the mood of the dreamer are of vital importance. To open a window in your dream can symbolise opening oneself to the influences of the world. A stained-glass window can have connotations of a pattern to the dreamer's life as well as the more obvious religious symbolism.

Witness If, in your dream, you seem to be a passive, or even captive, witness to some event, possibly a horrifying one, this could symbolise your feeling of helplessness in the face of superior force or maturity.

Woman (unknown to the dreamer) This dream, according to C.G. Jung, occurring only in men, can represent the personification of the dreamer's unconscious.

Work Dreaming of getting up and going to work in the morning, contrary to what you might think, can indicate reluctance – rather than eagerness – to get on with some necessary, but possibly unpleasant, task.

Wounds (scars, bleeding, etc.) However realistic, these are symbolic rather than literal injuries which indicate psychic or emotional damage brought to your attention by the subconscious.

I have another recurring dream; it is a visitation to a house, which by now I know very well. The rooms I could describe totally and in fact so well do I know them that I seem to rearrange furniture from my existing house within them, in the course of the dream. It is never a surprise to me when I visit this house because nocturnally I have spent so much time within it!

— *Derek Nimmo*

X

Xenophobia A dream in which you feel menaced or threatened by strangers or foreigners for no reason could indicate that you feel that some important area of your life – emotional, most likely – is being invaded by 'outsiders'.

X-ray X-ray vision, the ability to see through matter, is a common symbol for the dreamer's desire to 'see through' some thing or person or situation which seems to you to obscure or hide the truth.

Y

Yard A symbol for barrenness and lack of display (the opposite of a garden) the yard as a venue for a dream can indicate the dreamer's desire to get down to basics without pretence or ostentation.

Yardstick Though somewhat antiquated and superseded by tape measures, the yardstick still stands as a metaphor for assessment and measurement of the unknown. In a dream, the presence of a yardstick can symbolise the dreamer's need to apply a 'yardstick' or reliable standard to some as yet unquantified area of waking life.

Yarn (or wool) A symbol of transition. Yarn is a midway point between the raw material and the finished garment and as such can represent something in the dreamer's life which has not yet come to maturation, which has yet to take on its final configuration.

Yawn The phenomenon of repeated and perhaps involuntary yawning in one's dream can indicate that the dreamer feels a spiritual or intellectual 'tiredness'.

Yeast This is an important symbol of ferment and growth. If in your

Before his famous siege of Tyre, Alexander the Great dreamed of a satyr. Aristandros, his dream interpreter, broke the dream into two elements: *sa*, Greek for *your*, and *Tyros*, the name of the besieged city, and took the dream for a prophecy that Alexander would succeed in his mission.

dream a pot or cauldron of yeast is bubbling, this could be an indication that something in your waking life is in ferment and an important change in your circumstances could result.

Yield If in your dream you are forced to yield to some strong being or omnipotent force, this could symbolise your waking concern about a threat to your independence.

Yoga A quasi-religious symbol for dedication and discipline. The presence of practitioners of yoga in your dream could indicate that you feel that your own life is lacking in these qualities.

Yoke The presence of a yoke or yoked beasts – such as oxen or cattle – in your dream may symbolise your feeling that you need to be liberated from some onerous regime which you feel is inhibiting your personal freedom. A broken yoke could be a sign of liberation or of a bond broken in your waking life.

Youth It is axiomatic that a very youthful figure in your dream is almost certainly yourself, if not at an earlier age then representing the side of your personality and unconscious that has not aged, which will be forever youthful.

Yo-yo Though on the surface merely a toy, the yo-yo has become a popular symbol for rising and falling expectations and the mixed fortunes of life. If the yo-yo tangles or fails to rise, this could be an indication of some disappointment in your emotional or professional life.

Cooper Says...

I am not prone to having dreams, however one day last week I had a dream that I was wide awake, but when I woke up, there I was fast asleep!!

– *Henry Cooper*

Z

Zeal If in your dreams you seem to be feeling an extraordinary amount of energy and ambition toward some particular – if cloudy – goal, this may be an indication that you feel the lack of this zeal in your waking life, that you feel you are drifting rather than heading towards a goal.

Zebra A symbol of the mix of the routine and the exotic, a zebra out of context in your dream could indicate that you feel, underneath, you are very different from those around you.

Zeppelin A magical symbol of silence and awesome size, the appearance of a zeppelin or similar craft in your dream could represent the everlasting presence of conscience and a reminder that no act goes unobserved.

Zero Not the number, but the stark and dramatic Japanese fighter plane of World War II with its rising sun emblem, this is a symbol of surprise and evil and could suggest that the dreamer is

fearful of someone or something especially exotic in waking life.

Zeus A classic symbol of godliness, the figure of Zeus (as he is traditionally envisioned) in your dream will almost always represent someone to whom you accord great authority – your father, a teacher, your employer.

Zigzag A line in your dream which refuses to run straight but zigzags from side to side could well be a symbol for your feeling that your current activities or occupation is getting you nowhere in a hurry.

Zoo A symbol of confinement, like a prison but with the added element of public scrutiny. If you dream that you are in a zoo – especially if you are in a cage – this could indicate that you feel that in some of your behaviour

---

The night before [the parents of Alexander the Great] lay in wedded bed, the bride dreamed that lightning fell into her belly and that withal there was a great light fire that dispersed itself all about into divers flames. King Philip, her husband, also shortly after he was married, dreamed that he did seal his wife's belly, and that the seal bore the print of a lion. Certain wizards and soothsayers told Philip that this dream gave him warning to look straightly at his wife. But Aristander Telmesian answered against that it signified that Philip's wife was conceived with child and that she would give birth to a boy which should have the heart of a lion.

– from Plutarch's Life of Alexander the Great

Commentary

I commonly have anxiety dreams which are usually in the theme of missed deadlines or, when life gets very complicated, I sometimes have a dream that I am snookered and there is no way out of it, although at first glance there seem to be a number of possible escape routes. Although cricket is a sport I never cover I once dreamt that I was due to phone in a newpaper report from the Edgbaston Cricket Ground, which is near my office, but that I was stuck in an immovable traffic jam as the deadline passed. Shortly afterwards, I was commenting for the BBC on the World Snooker Championship from Sheffield where morning sessions begin at 10.30. The traffic outside my hotel in variably wakes me up shortly after 8.00 so I do not bother with a wake-up call. One morning, I woke up and casually looked at my watch. It was 10.25. Unshaven, I ran all the way to the theatre – no mean feat in my condition – but the session had already started. Fortunately one of the other commentators had shown up and had taken my place, so there was no great harm done. I wonder, though, whether my dream and this incident were connected.

– Clive Everton

you have displayed your animal nature to the cost of the human side.

Zulu A potent image suggesting primitive vigour and exotic menace, the presence of a Zulu warrior in your dream could represent your hidden capacity for action which is hidden and repressed by your more normal demeanour and occupation.

Zombie A standard symbol for mindless obedience and lack of self-will, if there is a zombie in your dream it is very likely your unconscious view of yourself as lacking independence and resolve in some matter which is important to you.

Bibliography

Some books which might give you a better insight into how dreams have been perceived by their examiners and interpreters through the ages.

De La Mare, Walter, *Behold this Dreamer*, Faber, London 1939.

Feud, Sigmund, *The Interpretation of Dreams*, Hogarth Press, London, 1953.

Fromm, Ernest, *The Forgotten Language*, Gollancz, London, 1952.

Hall, C. S., *The Meaning of Dreams*, Dell, New York, 1959.

Jung, Carl Gustav, *Collected Works*, Vols. 4, 16, Routledge, London, 1961.

Luce, G. G., and Segal, J., *Sleep* (Chapter 10), Heinemann, London, 1967.

Snyder, Franz, 'The New Biology of Dreams', *Archives of General Psychiatry* 8:381–391,1963.

Whitman, R. M., 'Remembering and forgetting Dreams in Psychanalysis', *Journal of the American Psychoanalysts' Association*, 7:752–774, 1963.

Woods, R. L., *The World of Dreams*, Random House, New York, 1947.

Facts and Figures

A recent survey revealed the extent of visual disability – 1.7 million adults in Britain have a sight problem. (Office of Population, Censuses and Surveys, 1988)

There are 223,000 adults registered blind or partially sighted in England, Scotland and Wales. (DHSS, 1986) However, we estimate that for every person registered another two are eligible.

More than one person in 20 over the age of 75 is severely visually handicapped.

Six in every 10 visually handicapped adults have another serious illness or disability. Many have more than one.

What is RNIB?

RNIB is Britain's largest organisation working for blind and partially sighted people. It is one of the biggest and best known charities in the UK.

Running our many services costs a great deal of money. In 1987/88 RNIB spent £31 million providing and improving services for visually handicapped people.

If you would like further information on any aspect of RNIB's work, or if you would like to make a donation, please complete with form below and send it to:

RNIB, 224 Great Portland Street,
London W1N 6AA. Telephone: 01-388 1266

- -

Name ....

Address ....

....

....

....

Blanket/Duvet Offer

For readers of this book, Dreamland will give a discount of £5 off the current suggested retail price of one of the blankets or duvets listed below and donate a similar sum to the RNIB.

   To take advantage of the offer, please write your name and address below, cut out this page, and send it to:

> Steven Bates
> Sales Administration Manager
> Yale and Valor Small Appliances
> Castle Malwood House
> Minstead
> Hampshire
> SO43 7NA

EM41P	Single, medium size electric underblanket with four heat levels and foot warmth.	£26.99
EM42P	Double, medium size electric under-blanket with four heat levels and foot warmth.	£33.99
EL42P	Single, large size electric underblanket with four heat levels and foot warmth.	£26.99
EL43P	Double, large size, dual control electric underblanket with four heat levels and foot warmth.	£42.99
DSD1	Single size electric Superduvet with variable heat control.	£59.99
DS43	Double size electric Superduvet with variable heat control and dual control.	£79.99
DSD4	Kingsize electric Superduvet with variable heat control and dual control.	£89.99

Prices are correct at time of book going to print.

The offer closes 31 August 1990.

Name ....

Address ....

....

....

....

DREAM RECORDING FORM

Date: _____ **Time (if known):** _____

What happened:_____

_____

_____

_____

_____

_____

Dream Details:

Day or night? _____ Season, if any? _____

Predominant colours recalled: _____

_____

Primary emotions recalled:_____

_____

_____

Physical sensations (if any): _____

_____

Familiar persons, animals, objects: _____

_____

_____

Miscellaneous: _____

_____

Mood on awakening: _____

_____

_____

_____

DREAM RECORDING FORM

Date: _____ **Time (if known):** _____

What happened: _____

_____

_____

_____

_____

_____

Dream Details:

Day or night? _____ Season, if any? _____

Predominant colours recalled: _____

_____

Primary emotions recalled: _____

_____

_____

Physical sensations (if any): _____

_____

Familiar persons, animals, objects: _____

_____

_____

Miscellaneous: _____

_____

Mood on awakening: _____

_____

_____

_____

DREAM RECORDING FORM

Date: _____ **Time (if known):** _____
What happened: _____
_____
_____
_____
_____
_____

Dream Details:
Day or night? _____ Season, if any? _____
Predominant colours recalled: _____
_____

Primary emotions recalled: _____
_____

Physical sensations (if any): _____
_____

Familiar persons, animals, objects: _____
_____

Miscellaneous: _____

Mood on awakening: _____
_____
_____
_____